DONALD SMITH is a storyteller of Scotland and noted performer. Inspired by his time at the School of Scottish Studies in Edinburgh, where he researched the pioneer feminist Naomi Mitchison, Donald became Director of The Netherbow Arts Centre and founding Director of the Scottish Storytelling Centre. In 2023 he received the Hamish Henderson Award for lifetime service to the Scottish arts. He is a longstanding activist in Earth Charter International, and co-founder of The Earth Stories Collection.

By the same author:

The Scottish Stage: A National Theatre Company for Scotland, Candlemaker Press, 1994
The Edinburgh Old Town Pilgrim's Way, John Pearson Publishing, 1995
John Knox House: Gateway to Edinburgh's Old Town, John Donald Publishing, 1996
Celtic Travellers, Stationery Office, 1997
Storytelling Scotland: A Nation in Narrative, Polygon, 2001
The English Spy, Luath Press, 2007
God, the Poet, and the Devil: Robert Burns and Religion, Saint Andrew Press, 2008
Between Ourselves, Luath Press, 2009
That Was Now, Scottish Arts Council, 2009
Arthur's Seat, with Stuart McHardy, Luath Press, 2012
Ballad of the Five Marys, Luath Press, 2013
Calton Hill with Stuart McHardy, Luath Press, 2013
Freedom and Faith: A Question of Scottish Identity, Saint Andrew Press, 2013
Edinburgh Old Town, with John Fee, Luath Press, 2014
Scotland's Democracy Trail, with Stuart McHardy, Luath Press, 2014
A Pilgrim Guide to Scotland, Saint Andrew Press, 2015
Flora McIvor, Luath Press, 2017
Travelling the Tweed Dales, with Elspeth Turner, Luath Press, 2018
Wee Folk Tales in Scots, Luath Press, 2018
Folk Tales from the Garden, The History Press, 2021
Storm and Shore: A Bardsaga, Luath Press, 2022
Saut an Bluid: A Scotsaga, Luath Press, 2022

CONTRIBUTOR: *A History of Scottish Theatre*, Mainstream; *Scotland: A Concise Cultural History*, Mainstream; *Scottish Life and Society*, European Ethnology Centre; *Edinburgh Companion to Twentieth Century Scottish Literature*, EUP; *Edinburgh Companion to Scottish Drama*, EUP; *The Earth Stories Collection,* Asociacion Avalon Project and *Oxford Companion to Scottish Theatre*, OUP.

PLAYS: *The Blue Blanket,* 1987; *Farewell Miss Julie Logan,* 2000; *Memory Hill,* 2002; *Cradle King,* 2003 and 2016; *The Death of Arthur,* 2006; *Kidnapped: When Kilts Were Banned,* 2007–16; *Home to Neverland,* 2007–10; *Jekyll and Hyde: A Specimen,* 2008 and 2017, *Burns Roughcut,* 2010–16; *Leaving Iona,* 2014; *Playing Lear,* 2016; *The Laird's Big Breaxit,* 2018; *Tour to the Hebrides,* 2020; *The Laird Strikes Back,* 2021.

Edinburgh

Our Storied Town

DONALD SMITH

Illustrations by Cat Outram

Luath Press Limited

EDINBURGH

www.luath.co.uk

First published 2024

ISBN: 978-1-80425-150-8 standard edition
ISBN: 978-1-80425-180-5 special edition

EDINBURGH **900**

The paper used in this book is recyclable. It is made from low-chlorine pulps
produced in a low-energy, low-emission manner from renewable forests.

Printed and bound by
CPI Antony Rowe Ltd., Chippenham

Typeset in 11 point Sabon by
Main Point Books, Edinburgh

Contents

For Alison
We twa hae rin aboot the braes
An pou'ed the gowans fine

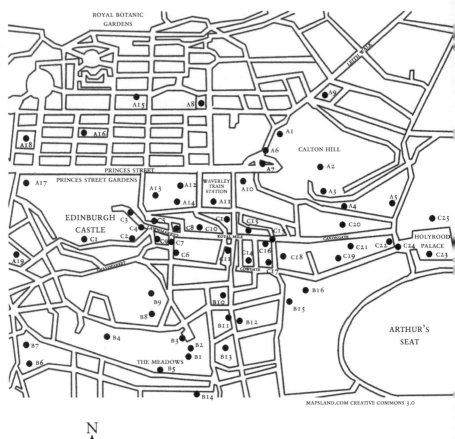

ROYAL BOTANIC
GARDENS

A15   A8

A16

A18   A1
                          A6   CALTON HILL
PRINCES STREET   A7
A17   PRINCES STREET GARDENS   A2
                A13   A12   WAVERLEY   A10
                              TRAIN
                A14   STATION   A11   A3
                                                A5
EDINBURGH   C3   C5   A4
CASTLE   C4 LAWNMARKET C8 C10 C1   C20   C25
      C1   C2   C9   C7   ROYAL MILE C13 C15   C21 C22 C24 HOLYROOD
A19   C6   C11   C14 C16   C19   PALACE
                              C17 C18   C23
                      COWGATE
                                          B16
            B9   B10   B15
      B8   ARTHUR'S
B4   B3   SEAT
            B2   B11 B12
      B7   B1
B6   THE MEADOWS B13
            B5

      B14
                        MAPSLAND.COM CREATIVE COMMONS 3.0

N

W ——→ E

S

Princes Street and New Town

A1 Playhouse Theatre
A2 Calton Hill
A3 Old Royal High School
A4 Burns Monument
A5 Calton Burial Ground
A6 Top of Leith Walk
A7 Sherlock Holmes statue
A8 Scottish National Portrait Gallery
A9 Elm Row – site of Gateway Theatre
A10 Old GPO – site of Theatre Royal
A11 Waverley Station
A12 Scott Monument
A13 National Gallery of Scotland
A14 Allan Ramsay statue (foot of Mound)
A15 17 Heriot Row – RL Stevenson birthplace
A16 39 North Castle Street – Sir Walter Scott's House
A17 St Cuthbert's Church
A18 Charlotte Square
A19 Royal Lyceum Theatre

Southside

B1 George Square
B2 Charles Street – site of Paperback Bookshop
B3 McEwan Hall
B4 Futures Institute Quartermile
B5 Meadows
B6 Bruntsfield Links – site of Muriel Spark's school
B7 Kings Theatre
B8 Sandy Bells Bar
B9 Greyfriars Kirkyard
B10 Old College – site of Kirk O' Field
B11 Festival Theatre
B12 Surgeons Hall
B13 Potterow/Nicolson Square – site of Clarinda's house
B14 Sciennes Hill Place – Adam Ferguson's House
B15 Pleasance Theatre
B16 St John's Hill – site of James Hutton's house

Old Town/Royal Mile

C1 Edinburgh Castle – St Margaret's Chapel
C2 Scottish National War Memorial
C3 Ramsay Gardens
C4 Outlook Tower
   Edinburgh Festival Hub
   The General Assembly Hall
   Riddle's Court
   Gladstone's Land
   St James' Court – site of Traverse
   Theatre Club
   Makars Court
C5 The Writers Museum
C6 National Library of Scotland
C7 Central Library
C8 David Hume Statue
C9 St Giles Cathedral
   Site of 'Heart of Midlothian'
   John Knox's Grave – lot 23 Parliament Square
C10 Adam Smith Statue
C11 Tron Square – west side – site of George
      Buchanan's house
C12 Fleshmarket Close

C13 Carrubber's Close – site of Allan Ramsay's Theatre
    John Knox House
    Scottish Book Trust
    Patrick Geddes Sculpture (Sandeman House Garden)
C14 Blackfriars Street
    Site of Chepman and Myllar's
      printers – foot of Blackfriars Street
C15 Site of The Netherbow Port
C16 Tweeddale Court
C17 The Saltire Society
C18 Chessel's Court
C19 Moray House – site of Canongate Playhouse
C20 Canongate Kirkyard
    Robert Fergusson Sculpture
C21 Scottish Poetry Library
C22 Scottish Parliament
    Wall of Quotes
C23 Holyroodhouse Palace
C24 Holyrood Abbey
C25 St Margaret's Well

Preface and Acknowledgements

Edinburgh: Our Storied Town has been written as a contribution to the 900th anniversary of Edinburgh as a royal burgh in 2024, which also marks 20 years since the city became the world's first UNESCO City of Literature. Edinburgh is a unique, creative place, a prime focus for Scotland's literature, history and culture. This book weaves all these threads into one narrative tapestry. I would like to thank the teams behind both anniversaries for their support, as well as all at Luath Press, my wonderful illustrator, Cat Outram, and my colleagues at the Scottish International Storytelling Festival, TRACS and Festivals Edinburgh, without whom this book could not have happened.

Sources in copyright used with permission and under Fair Dealing rules are endnoted. Out-of-copyright quotations are drawn from open sources, principally Project Gutenburg and the Internet Archive. Scots orthography has been adapted for accessibility and Latin and Gaelic texts re-translated. I also acknowledge the superb research on Scottish Literature carried out in the last 50 years. You will find more information about these studies, anthologies and editions in the Further Reading section at the end of the book.

I have learned a lot from this research, but even more from writers, storytellers, adaptors, actors, radio producers and filmmakers in my 50 years of association with the Scottish Storytelling Centre, formerly The Netherbow, in Edinburgh. Through creative media, I have explored many of the texts and authors discussed here. Sometimes I feel they have become familiar friends, who have deepened my own sense of life and its challenges. My hope is that you might feel equally enriched.

Every so often you hit on a book that changes the way you look at things. Scottish writers are a diverse, forward-thinking community and in writing this book my thoughts have been changed by John MacQueen's *Ballatis of Luve* (Edinburgh University Press, 1970); George Davie's *The Scottish Enlightenment* with a foreword by James Kelman (Polygon, 1990); *Sorley MacLean: Critical Essays* edited by Raymond J Ross and Joy Hendry (Scottish Academic Press, 1986), DER Watt's selections from Walter Bower in *A History Book for Scots* (Birlinn, 2019); Elizabeth Jay's *Mrs Oliphant: A Fiction to Herself* (Clarendon Press, 1995); Kate Phillips' *Bought & Sold: Scotland, Jamaica and Slavery* (Luath Press, 2022) and David Pollock's *Edinburgh's Festivals: A Biography* (Luath Press, 2023). All of these books throw new light on important subjects, and I am grateful for their insights.

Introduction

THIS BOOK IS an invitation to explore. It is for readers, writers and all those who are interested in how those activities interact with a sense of place. Anyone who loves Edinburgh should also dip in, because through its nine official centuries, this city has thrived on books, words and ideas. In times of change and crisis the distinction between a Scottish writer and one distinctive to Edinburgh and the eastern Lowlands becomes blurred. At different points, I cover both to make sense of the overall picture.

Edinburgh is much older than 900 years, but 1124 marks the first document which confirms its status as a royal burgh. It is an interesting date, coinciding with the growth of written literature and the start of Edinburgh's journey towards becoming Scotland's capital.

The city's character is, however, founded on something more fundamental and prehistoric – its geology. This contributes not only the castle rock, which provided an ancient fortress, but the compact identity of a town which rests on an extinct volcano. The result combines surprising vistas with a diversity of intimate nooks and crannies, within metres of each other.

Architects have revelled in this urban identity, creating indoor and outdoor spaces that foster sociability, while also harbouring privacy. And that is how culture bubbles up with congenial possibilities for sharing ideas and experiences, alongside places for solitary reflections and dreams.

Edinburgh: Our Storied Town works broadly by centuries, but within each time period there is a focus on different forms of literature, and on some individual writers as artistic characters of continuing interest. The book is not a history lesson, though key background events are described. Rather, it engages with writers and texts that deserve to be read, without presuming prior knowledge. In reading, you join a continuing story which is still being created across the centuries. Literature is not trapped in the present tense.

Through many of these past centuries, women were not encouraged to be public writers. In some periods, repressive patriarchy persecuted women, yet in each century significant women have played a part. This is especially true of the earliest cultural layers, but a submerged richness of female voices continues as an integral part of the narrative until women claimed their equal public place to the huge benefit of literature.

Edinburgh's long literary heritage is visible in the city, and I reference this throughout the text. You could walk the book through Edinburgh, and stumble on new points of interest in a poetry of stone and bronze. The map and Timeline provide some additional prompts. Like Edinburgh's geology, this story has, thankfully, no prospect of an ending, though difficult challenges lie ahead for a city poised between land and sea.

ONE

Time Before Time: Myth and Legend

Sacred Landscape

LONG BEFORE EDINBURGH was accredited as a royal burgh, there was a fortress and settlement on the Castle Rock. The first name that has come down to us for this place is Din Eidyn, the fort of Eidyn. Who was Eidyn? God, king, hero, giant? We do not know, but the language is Cymric – what might now be called Old Welsh. Eidyn's fort was in the Celtic kingdom of Gododdin, which had come to terms with the Roman Province of Britannia, whose shifting northern frontier eventually settled at Hadrian's Wall.

Above Din Eidyn was what we now call Arthur's Seat. Again we are in a realm of gods and heroes, not medieval knights or holy grails. Like Benarty in Fife or Ben Arthur in Argyll, the rocky summit was literally a seat where the god could touch the heavens, especially, in Arthur's case, the Bear star, Arcturus. Like a hibernating bear, Arthur still sleeps below his mountains, waiting on the call to rescue his people.

So, remarkably, a sacred landscape sits in the centre of Edinburgh, with its hilltop seat and ascending terraces still visible. Beneath them is the holy water of Duddingston Loch – Trefyr Lin in Cymric – the settlement by the loch. Weapons and other metal offerings were cast in to the water as sacrifices, foreshadowing the myth of Arthur's sword Excalibur. The medieval Duddingston Kirk still looks over the loch from what is likely an ancient religious site.

In general, our oldest folklore is about how the landscape was formed. The forces of volcanic fire and then grinding ice which shaped Edinburgh are represented in this lore by a mother goddess or Cailleach (Carlin in Scots) and her rock-chucking giant children. Tradition tells us that this formidable giantess 'let fart Berwick Law'!

Later theories became more refined, but the core drama remains as land and sea, islands and hills, meet in a unique terrain. Arthur's Seat, the Castle Crag and Calton Hill are remnants of one huge volcano worn down by the ice. To the east, Traprain Law, formerly Dunpelder, and North Berwick Law stand proud on the coastal plain below the long, low range of the Moorfoot and Lammermuir hills. Seawards, Inchkeith, the Bass Rock and May Isle, which sits in the mouth of what was called the Scottish Sea, are prominent. To the north, the Lomonds' twin peaks – the Paps o Fife – complete the ensemble. From another angle, Edinburgh juts into the sea with Leith at its head, as if continuing the eastward run of the Pentlands which also extend westwards like a recumbent dragon.

The old stories, like later history and literature, are also formed by that interaction of sea and land. The legends of Edinburgh's 'Castle of the Maidens' nod across to the Isle of May or Maidens, blending Celtic priestesses with early Christian saints. It was the sea which brought the Romans to Edinburgh, establishing a major port and fortress at Caer Amon – now Cramond. Though the Romans remained an occupying power, never absorbing Scotland into their empire, they had great influence on the tributary kingdoms like Gododdin. Their most lasting legacy was the spread of Christianity, and the fort by the River Almond later housed a church.

A dramatic story from this period is best viewed from Arthur's

Seat. Tennoch or Thenew (later known as the biblical Enoch) was the daughter of Loth, king of Gododdin, who gave his name to the Lothians. He decreed that Tennoch should marry her cousin Owen, Prince of Strathclyde, sealing a royal alliance between the Cymric kingdoms. But she refused, having come under the influence of women missionaries from Ireland. They offered a radically different path for women in a patriarchal culture. Enraged by her disobedience, Loth sent Tennoch into the Lammermuirs to labour as a swineherd. But her resolve was unbroken.

Owen, the story relates, came to claim his rights as a betrothed Prince. Later hagiography piously beat about the bush, but rape ensued and Tennoch fell pregnant. But still she resisted marriage. She was brought back to Traprain Law and sentenced by Loth to death by stoning. But, in biblical mode, the people refused to carry out the cruel sentence. Next, Loth ordered her thrown from the cliff in a ritual chariot. But the axle did not break, and Tennoch reached the ground bruised but alive. Lastly, stubborn old Loth had her cast off into the Forth in a coracle without sail, oar, food or water – an especially cruel, slow death in Celtic culture.

But as the coracle drifted seawards out of Aberlady Bay, it was followed in procession by seals, fish and porpoises, so that no sea harvest was ever landed at Aberlady again. The coracle went out with the tide, but beached on the May Isle, where there was the freshwater Maidens Well. In this way, Tennoch survived until her little craft could be borne upriver by the tide, landing eventually in the darkness at Culross. She gave birth to her son on the beach, stirring the embers of a fish-smoking fire that had been smoored by the monks of St Serf's community. They found mother and baby alive in the morning.

The child became Kentigern, nicknamed Mungo, the founder of Glasgow. As for Tennoch, her wish to become a leader in the Celtic Church was fulfilled, and she founded a community of women on Inchcailloch in Loch Lomond. Her sacred well was in Glasgow Cathedral, and she was buried below what is still known as St Enoch's Square.

The same themes of sexual resistance and independence feature in the legend of St Triduana, a woman saint whose principal shrine and burial place was at Restalrig in Edinburgh. Triduana was remorselessly pursued by a Prince, till finally she demanded to know what part of her inflamed his desire. Her eyes, he replied, on which she pricked them out with a twig of thorns and handed them over. Subsequently, Triduana's healing work and her shrines were associated with diseases of the eye.

Triduana had chapels at Traprain, Rescobie in Angus and Papa Westray in Orkney. She may have been the same person as St Medana or Monenna in the Mull of Galloway, and this Saint is connected to the Chapel of the Maidens in Edinburgh Castle. Yet another legend in this cluster has Medanna accompanying St Rule when he brought the relics of St Andrew from Greece to Kilrymont, later St Andrews. These are the shifting sands of storytelling, yet the consequences were real in memory and devotion. Even in the 16th century, pilgrims came to Restalrig in significant numbers, while St Margaret's Chapel in Edinburgh Castle, successor to the Maidens Chapel, is the city's oldest surviving church building.

The Gododdin

Back in the 6th and 7th centuries, Anglo-Saxons from the north European mainland moved into gaps left by the withdrawal of the Romans. They pushed up from Northumbria into southern Scotland, clashing with Gododdin and Strathclyde, as well as the Gaelic kingdom of Dalriada in Argyll. Edinburgh's earliest known poem laments the consequences of a great expedition south from Din Eidyn to repel the Saxon invaders.

Warriors from across the Cymric kingdoms gathered to train and feast at Din Eidyn before riding south to a disastrous but heroic defeat. The Gododdin poem, composed by the famous bard Aneirin, laments each of the fallen heroes and contains the first known reference in written literature to Arthur, already a legendary war leader of earlier times. 'Though he was not Arthur,' declaims Aneirin, 'Gwarddur was the first line's bulwark, and brought black crows to the fort's wall.' However, 'weariness descended like death', and like so many others he fell in the battle.

The Gododdin was probably composed in the 590s soon after the events described, which include Aneirin's own escape from captivity after the fight. Edinburgh was captured by the Anglo-Saxons in 638 and was absorbed into Northumbria for a period, leading to the widespread confusion that Edinburgh's name means (King) 'Edwin's burgh'. The poem survived through traditions of 'the Men of the North' which migrated south to Wales, and later through written manuscripts, the oldest of which is in the care of Cardiff City Council.

The era of Northumbrian power brought new cultural and religious influences, including the founding of a church in Edinburgh by St Cuthbert. His birth and upbringing in the Scottish Borders combined Celtic and Saxon traditions in attractive spirituality. He personally founded many churches including one below Edinburgh Castle in the West End, and perhaps another on the site of what is now Colinton Parish Church. Many other churches were later dedicated to this popular saint whose unworldly love of solitude and the natural world endeared him to succeeding generations. The founding of St Giles Church in Edinburgh belongs to a later period and is connected with the town's growth as a centre of trade.

Writing Saint Margaret

A shift from legend towards history is associated with the 11th century life of Saint Margaret of Scotland, another powerful woman in Edinburgh's early story. The shift is marked by an increased use of written manuscripts, and the growing status of literacy gradually displacing the respect accorded to oral tradition in Celtic culture. It is with Margaret that Edinburgh's strictly literary history begins.

This is evident in Margaret's own devotion to her illuminated Gospel book, which she used as a focus for contemplation in the style brought from the Mediterranean world by Irish and then Benedictine monks. Margaret was distressed when this book was lost crossing a stream on one of the royal court's many journeys. Remarkably, the book was found and restored to its thankful owner with minimal damage. A Gospel book associated with Margaret, marked with water stains, is preserved in the Bodleian Library in Oxford.

The spread of literacy brought more than an increase in written texts; it also caused new narrative forms to emerge. This included the Lives of Saints, modelled on exemplars from the classical world such as Athanasius' *Life of Saint Anthony*, the desert hermit. A notable early Scottish example was Abbot Adomnan's *Life of Columba*, which was composed in Latin, marking the centenary of Columba's death in 597. This is an outstanding book, still widely read, with a claim to be the first major work of Scottish Literature.

Like many of the genre, Adomnan's *Life of Columba* is not a chronological account of the subject's life. Adomnan drew on earlier traditions kept alive on Iona, but he developed his own sections of prophecies, visions and miracles, all culminating in the beloved Columba's death. This is relayed as an island pilgrimage, establishing the holy places of Iona like those of Jerusalem.

Written books bring with them individual authors and editors whose viewpoints may narrow the more fluid interpretations of oral tradition. This is especially true of the surviving *Life of Saint Margaret* by her confessor and adviser Turgot, a Benedictine monk from Durham. Although Turgot relates that before Margaret died she told him the whole story of her life, he is more interested in her public role as a religious reformer. While acknowledging her learning, personal devotion and charitable support for orphans, the poor and prisoners of war, the Benedictine allocates most space to Margaret's efforts to improve (to his eyes) defective Scottish customs by replacing them with English models. The picture he paints is of a bossy woman insisting on rule changes that seem petty beside the big issues that Margaret actually tackled.

By taking this ecclesiastical angle, Turgot excludes much of Margaret's early life. Her family had fled persecution in England,

and she was born in Hungary to Agatha, a Hungarian royal. He skips over her exceptional education in Hungary and subsequently at the court of Edward the Confessor in Westminster, and then plays down the family's renewed flight following the conquest of England by Duke William of Normandy. Finally, Turgot has almost nothing to say about Margaret's husband, Malcolm III, King of Scots. He had himself spent a long exile in England after his father, King Duncan, was killed and supplanted by Macbeth, but then courageously recovered his throne with help from England.

Fortunately, the *Anglo-Saxon Chronicle* pays much more attention to these major matters, possibly incorporating material from another lost Life of Margaret. The *Chronicle* emphasises Margaret's desire to fulfil her education by leading a devout religious life, perhaps as an Abbess. By contrast, Malcolm is determined to win her as his Queen, quietly banishing an existing Norse wife, Ingrid. In the end, says the *Chronicle*, Margaret gave way in order to fulfil God's will that she should turn the Scottish kingdom towards 'true religion'.

Many other interesting things about Margaret emerge from different sources. While founding a fine new church and monastery at Dunfermline, Malcolm and Margaret increasingly used Edinburgh as a centre of government. This included construction of a timber chapel in Edinburgh Castle, which Margaret's son David converted to the stone building that still stands today. Margaret also supported the restoration of a Culdee (Companions of God) community on Iona. It is clear that Margaret combined her support for new European expressions of Christianity with a reverence for older patterns of devotion. By providing a ferry for pilgrims to St Andrews and pilgrim hostels on both sides of the Queensferry,

Margaret helped renew an ancient Celtic shrine with a strengthened cult of St Andrew.

Margaret's childhood and youth had been threatened by wars, and her old age was no different. She died besieged in Edinburgh Castle after Malcolm and her oldest son, Edward, had been killed in an ambush in Northumbria. She kept beside her a fragment of the true cross, her most precious relic, which was mounted in gold and silver and cased in ebony – the Haly Rude. She died in the castle and, according to what may be legendary embellishment, her body had to be lowered from the battlements and conveyed secretly across the Forth for burial at Dunfermline.

These events were, however, the beginning rather than the end of Margaret's story and influence. In 1250, she became Scotland's first officially canonised saint, and a rare example of a saint who had been a wife and mother. Pope Innocent IV, with some input from the Scottish bishops, rose to the occasion, putting Turgot to shame.

A precious pearl saw the light in Hungary, and lived at the court of the Confessor, a School of Holiness. Torn from homeland, you embrace another. You became Queen and Mother, the glory of Scots. Your Queen's crown, a crown of Charity. Your way, the Royal Way of the Cross. Once, mere men, placed crowns upon your head. But I, Innocent, Peter's successor, Servant of Christ, now place upon your head, the greatest crown of all, sainthood.

In consequence, Margaret's body was moved to a new shrine behind the high altar at Dunfermline Abbey. When her tomb was opened, according to *The Book of Pluscarden*, a monastic chronicle, the church was filled with the fragrance of flowers. Her remains were placed in a reliquary adorned with precious metals and borne towards the high altar with chants and hymns. But as the procession passed Malcolm's tomb, the reliquary became unbearably heavy and had to be lowered to the ground. Then someone made the inspired suggestion that Malcom's remains should also be moved to the new shrine, beside his Queen. Now the burden was lightened and husband and wife were reburied, mutually beloved in death as in life.

Three of Margaret's children reigned as kings of Scots, culminating in the rule of David I. Her daughter Matilda married Henry I of England and, like Margaret, proved an effective ruler alongside her husband. Margaret's younger daughter Maud married Count Eustace of Boulogne, and between them her children ensured that many of Europe's royal houses could claim some descent from the saintly Queen.

The legends also multiplied. On Holy Cross Day 1127, King David went hunting against the advice of his counsellors. Coming on a white stag in the royal hunting park at Arthur's Seat, David pursued his quarry and outrode his companions. Amidst bushes and low trees, the stag turned at bay. The King's horse reared in fright and threw David. Then the stag lowered his antlers and charged. David reached out to ward off the sharp tines but found himself holding a cross. That night he had a dream vision that he should found an abbey near that spot in memory of his mother, Margaret, and her Haly Rude or Cross. So Holyrood Abbey came into being.

Close by the Abbey, in what was the royal hunting park, is St Margaret's Well, the housing of which was brought from St

Triduana's Well on the pilgrim path to Restalrig. That route has recently been reopened as part of the development of Meadowbank Stadium. The old paths can be resilient through Edinburgh's centuries.

TWO

Measuring Time: Chronicle and Saga

The Rise of Paperwork

QUEEN MARGARET DIED in 1093, and in the following 200 years her successors realised her dream of Scotland as a European Christian kingdom. Her youngest son David, who ruled from 1124 to 1153, proved to be an outstanding administrator and reformer, whose generous financial support of the Church earned him the tag – 'ane sair sanct for the croun'.

David's reign generated more documentation than ever, and it is no coincidence that charters confirming Edinburgh's status as a royal burgh and St Giles as the burgh church are both dated 1124. Holyrood Abbey followed in 1128, as the new king's reign gathered pace. Taken together, these developments underline the growing importance of Edinburgh, though Dunfermline continued to be of high value as the royal dynasty's principal shrine.

Documentary records reinforced the status of the written word in this reforming kingdom, and also led to more recording of historical events. This work was carried out by churchmen, who were by definition 'the clerics'. Some worked as part of the royal administration, but it was in the monasteries that chronicles were maintained. The monastic rules were dedicated to measuring time, so documenting by the calendar year came naturally. There may also have been a religious aspect to giving an account of events, and so justifying God's sometimes mysterious providence. Such documents might provide some form of witness on the Day of Judgement.

However, it is also true that the monks kept classical or secular books and manuscripts in their libraries. Some also recorded local tales and traditions which might otherwise have been lost. Theirs was a genuine love of book learning.

The early chronicles can be terse and yet portentous. The oldest Scottish chronicle was kept on Iona, but was moved to Ireland after the Viking attacks. These events were preserved in succeeding Irish annals.

794: Devastation of all the islands of Britain by the gentiles (Norsemen).
806: The Community of Iona was slain by the gentiles, that is to say sixty-eight monks.

So began the enormous impact of Norse raiding, settlement, war and trade on England, Ireland and Scotland.

The *Anglo-Saxon Chronicle*, though still concise, becomes more descriptive about events in Scotland, as in 1054:

This year went Siward the Earl with a great army into Scotland, both with a ship-force and a land-force, and fought against the Scots, and put to flight King Macbeth, and slew all who were the chief men in the land. And had there much booty, such as no man had obtained.

Concealed in this account is the restoration of Malcolm Canmore's line to the Scottish throne.

The *Chronicle* is a contemporary witness of the struggle for England between Danish and sometimes Norwegian forces on the one hand, and the royal Saxon house of Wessex on the other. This battle was settled by a third party, the Norsemen or Normans from across the English Channel, in the shape of William the Conqueror. As already described, these events dramatically affected Margaret and her family, the Athelings, bringing her in due course to Scotland.

The Norse side of these conflicts also had notable chroniclers. Again, the earliest records can be terse, as in *Landnambok*, or *Book of the Settlements* in Iceland. These settlements became the third axis of a three-way movement of people between Norway, Scotland and the new north. The recording of events soon developed into vividly descriptive sagas, not least in the hands of Snorri Sturluson who is the first saga-man or woman to emerge as an individual author. His *Heimskringla: Lives of the Norse Kings* has a lot to say about Scotland.

> Then Thorstein Red, the son of Olaf White and Aud the Wealthy, came into an alliance with Earl Sigurd of Orkney. They raided in Scotland, and acquired Caithness and Sutherland, as far as the banks of Oykell.
>
> Earl Sigurd slew Maelbrighte TuskTooth, the Pictish Earl; and he bound Maelbrighte's head to his saddle straps, and grazed the calf of his leg upon the tooth which stuck out from the head. Swelling arose there and he got his death from it.

This grisly episode is dramatically expanded in *Orkneyinga Saga*, which provides a defining account of relationships between Norway, Scotland and Iceland. Events in the north were to continue to play a key part in Scotland's chronicles.

On the Scottish mainland, two important, composite chronicles were accumulated. The *Chronicles of the Kings of Scotland*, sometimes called the *Pictish Chronicles*, begin from an interest in how the dynasties of Pictland and the Gaelic stronghold of Dalriada came together to form one Scottish kingdom. The *Melrose Chronicle*, an ambitious southern account of Scotland, was maintained at Melrose Abbey, absorbing many other sources in verse and prose, including the *Book of Pluscarden*.

Both of these major sources show strong interest in the bloody sequence of events that brought Malcom Canmore to the Scottish throne. When the warlike and ruthless Malcom II died, he was succeeded by his son Duncan. But Duncan was overthrown in open battle by Macbeth, whose wife, Gruoch, had a claim to the Scottish throne through a line of descent in Moray. Duncan's son Malcolm, as we have recorded, went into a long exile in England, but was eventually put on the throne by Earl Siward of Northumbria's invasion. Macbeth was subsequently killed in a battle at Lumphanan in the northeast, but the succession was disputed until Macbeth's son Lulach was also killed in a skirmish at Strathbogie.

These early Scottish chronicles are clear that Macbeth's 17-year reign was a time of prosperity for Scotland. King Macbeth went on a pilgrimage to Rome, spread alms liberally and was buried with full regal honours on Iona. The Canmore dynasty fostered a different picture as the Men of Moray continued to be a thorn in their side. So emerged the murderous Macbeth and his treacherous wife, a story which was destined to run and run.

A Master Narrative

At this juncture, however, Macbeth is a subsidiary topic in the wider emergent narrative about Scotland's golden age as a medieval Christian kingdom ruled by the Canmores. This stretches from the saintly reign of Margaret with her husband through to the death of Alexander III in 1286. It is a story of war and piety, as Scotland expanded its frontiers south, north and west, while building a network of prestigious monasteries and churches across the realm.

In due course this master narrative would be enshrined in no less than three major chronicles, authored in sequence by Andrew of Wyntoun, Prior of St Serf's in Loch Leven; John of Fordun, a chantry priest at St Machar's Cathedral in Aberdeen; and Abbot Walter Bower of Inchcolm Abbey in the Forth. Bower's monumental *Scotichronicon* builds on the other two. Wyntoun wrote in Scots verse, while Fordun and Bower deployed Latin prose.

All three authors wrote much later than the earliest events they describe, but were spurred on by contemporary happenings. Fordun was gathering materials and writing in the 1370s and 1380s. Wyntoun worked between 1407 and 1420, while Abbot Bower began work in 1441 continuing until his death in 1449. In each case there is a desire to place the Scottish story within a wider universal framework provided by Christianity. This has a double-edged effect – subordinating the national narrative while also validating it by lending a sacred purpose.

These are individually authored works not compilations, though they do draw on a variety of earlier sources. Further, they have learned from the saga makers and poets, and from classical literature, how to be authoritative and entertain readers or listeners.

Fordun's account, for example, of Margaret's son Alexander I is grim and unadorned, stressing his warlike nature. But Bower is interested in Alexander's part in the founding of his own Inchcolm Abbey, and builds on the dramatic interaction between sea and land that characterises royal events.

Alexander, according to Bower, is caught in a fierce storm in the Forth and shipwrecked on Inchcolm. There he is given shelter by a hermit, perhaps one of the Culdees honoured by his mother. The storm continues unabated for some time, but eventually King Alexander is able to resume his journey. As a result of this experience he endows an Abbey for Inchcolm, which becomes 'the Iona of the East', while ensuring that a humble hermit's cell is retained in a quiet garden amongst the new buildings – where it can still be seen. 'The King and the Hermit' has all the features of saintly folklore, but is also germane to Bower's core purpose.

Crusading Legends

A similar embroidering takes place around David I and the Crusades. Both Fordun and Wyntoun retain a tradition that, during the long reign of his elder brother William the Lion, Prince David went on crusade. There is no other evidence to back this up, but Abbot Bower, drawing on the eulogy of David by Aelred of Rievaulx, stresses that when David became king he wanted to abdicate and go on crusade. He then had to be dissuaded by his religious advisers, and by 'the tears of the poor, the groans of widows, the desolation of the people, and the outcry and lamentation of the whole kingdom'. Nonetheless, continues Bower, he was held back 'bodily, not by his mind or will'. This situation is confirmed by

David's strong support for the Knights Templar, the crusading order, which he kept close as 'guardians of his morals by night and day'.

Bower's account smacks of hagiography, but it is backed up by the number of properties belonging to the crusading orders in the Edinburgh area during this period. The Templars were given lands to establish preceptories in Temple Liston (now Kirkliston) and at Temple in Midlothian. The Knights Hospitaller of St John were based at Torphichen in West Lothian and owned land in the Canongate, still known as St John's Street.

Knights from many landed families went on crusade from religious or mercenary motives, or a mixture of the two. The Statutes of the Scottish Church endorse the Crusades in obedience to the Lateran Council in Rome, but show awareness of mixed motives.

> We also ordain by authority of the Lateran Council that
> Crusaders are to be duly protected by the Church, unless
> for the heinousness of their crimes, they have been disbarred
> from ecclesiastical protection.

In the longer term, the Crusades were an unedifying chapter in the history of Christendom, despite the idealism with which things began.

There may also be a crusading link in the dedication of Edinburgh's principal church to St Giles. The crusading land route south went down the Rhône valley where St Giles was connected with Arles and Nîmes. Greek in origin, Giles was a protector of lepers, the weak and the disabled. In one famous incident he protected a deer hind, who had offered him her milk, from hunters. He took an arrow in his leg leaving him permanently lame.

According to Aelred of Rievaulx, David I's friend and hagiographer, a younger David had been urged by his sister Queen Matilda to follow St Giles' example by washing and kissing the feet of lepers in London. But he fled from the task. Edinburgh's coat of arms had two heraldic supporters – St Giles with his injured leg bared and a deer. After the Protestant Reformation, Giles was replaced with a maiden, but in representations such as that on The Netherbow Bell of 1621, she still has a giveaway leg bared.

Sir Walter Scott was to scoop up the legends of Scottish Crusaders in his 19th-century novel *The Talisman,* a companion piece to his English medieval novel *Ivanhoe.* By that time, Romanticism had purged the Crusades of their brutal reality.

Tragic Endings

Norse sagas also continued to be relevant to Scotland's master narrative, as both Alexander II and Alexander III battled to gain control of the Western Isles from Norway. This was gradually settled following the indecisive Battle of Largs in 1263. Though more a skirmish than a full-scale battle, Largs ended King Haakon of Norway's great Scottish expedition, and he died in Orkney on the way home.

The eventual treaty between Scotland and Norway included a marriage alliance between the two royal houses. This led in due course to Princess Margaret, the Maid of Norway, being the last direct descendant of Malcom and Margaret in line for the Scottish crown.

As for Largs itself, Abbot Bower expanded on another story from the *Book of Pluscarden* in which, according to the testimony of 'a monk from Dunfermline', Sir John Wemyss, a noble knight of Fife experienced a vision on the eve of the battle. As he stood at the door of Dunfermline Abbey, a lady of radiant beauty emerged from the church with a fully armoured knight on her arm. He wore a crown on his helmet and was followed by three other knights. 'Who are you, Glorious Lady, and where are you going?' ventured Wemyss.

> 'I am Margaret, formerly Queen of Scots. The knight who has my arm is the lord King Malcolm my husband, and these knights who are following us are our sons, the most renowned kings of this realm while they lived. In company with them I am hurrying to defend our country at Largs, and to win a victory over the usurper who is unjustly trying to make my kingdom subject to his rule. For you must know that I received this kingdom from God, granted in trust to me and to our heirs for ever.'

Dream visions are the stuff of medieval poetry, but Bower uses this example to neatly encapsulate the master narrative: Margaret is still the guiding spirit of this Christian kingdom.

Largs is a high point in the narrative curve, but Bower is also prepping us for tragic reverse. He builds up to this with consummate storytelling skill, going beyond his predecessors and applying saga-style portents and prophecies with a liberal hand. The problem was, as ever, about royal succession. Alexander III had only one surviving child, by his first marriage to Princess Margaret of England. She was the Margaret of Scotland who had been married off to Haakon's grandson Eric of Norway as part of the post-Largs settlement. In 1275 Alexander's spouse, Margaret, died, leaving him without male heirs.

In 1285 Yolande de Dreux, a young French noblewoman, came to Scotland with an aristocratic retinue to marry Alexander. This was a fine French alliance to balance the close relationship with England, and a new start for royal fecundity. A magnificent feast was hosted at Jedburgh with hunting in the forest by day, and dance, storytelling and music by night. A rowdy court masque was led by bagpipers, but last in the procession came a ghostly apparition gliding above the ground. Everyone stopped to gape but the figure disappeared into thin air. The frenzied procession halted, the music faded and the dancers froze suddenly and unexpectedly. The party was revived, but a skull-like shadow of ill-omen lingered. The following year, Queen Margaret of Norway died in childbirth leaving an infant daughter as heir to Scotland.

Six months on from the Jedburgh feast, on 19th May 1286, Alexander crossed the Forth at the Queensferry in rough weather to join his young bride at their manor in Kinghorn. He was strongly advised to travel no further that night, but impetuously he took the waiting horses and set off through the worsening storm with a small escort.

The previous day, back in the Scottish Borders, Thomas of Ercildoune, also known as Thomas the Rhymer, had warned the Earl of March that the next day, when the Earl planned to hunt, a great wind of calamity would strike Scotland. 'The like of this,' said Thomas, 'has not been known since former times.' But the next day dawned fair, and the Earl and his companions chafed Thomas for his unfulfilled prophecy. Then the Rhymer repeated his doom-laden foreknowledge and claimed that the coming blast would 'dumbfound the nation'.

The Earl's company went inside to eat when a loud, urgent knocking sounded on the outer door. A messenger was let in, and blurted out the news of Alexander's death. The king had been thrown by his horse on the rocks above Kinghorn beach, close to his destination. An extended trauma lay ahead for the Scots, since Alexander's untimely death opened the door to Edward I of England's imperial ambitions and his attempt, in due course, to erase Scotland as an independent nation.

The storytelling impulse is often linked to some form of disruption or discontinuity which the narrator seeks to mend through re-connecting stories.

This motivation applies to all three of our master narrators – Fordun, Wyntoun and Bower. In fact, Fordun began his quest travelling in search of documentary records to fill the gaps left by Edward I's removal of Scotland's state papers to London. This was as damaging as the symbolic loss of the Stone of Destiny on which Scottish rulers had been inaugurated, though whether Edward got hold of the real Stone or an inferior substitute remains a debated point.

In this collective effort to re-connect, our chroniclers were to be joined by epic poets, minstrels and writers of Romance in fashioning an alternative narrative for Scotland – one of heroic resistance and survival.

THREE

13th and 14th Century: Epic and Romance

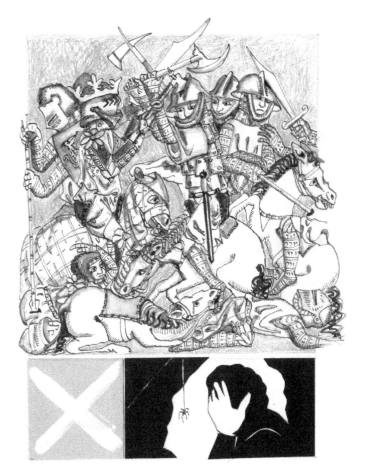

National Crisis

When Alexander our kynge was dede
That lede in lauche (law) and le (protection)
Away was sons (plenty) of alle and brede
Of wyne and wax, gamyn and gle.
Our gold was changit into lede.
Christ, borne in virgynyte,
Succoure Scotland, and remede,
That stade is in perplexitie.

THE IMMEDIATE REACTION to Alexander III's death was one of raw emotion and lament. The golden age had ended. Thomas of Erceldoune's prophecy of a blast that would dumbfound the nation proved correct, with a wave of aftershocks added. The Guardians, or Regents, of Scotland sent immediately for Princess Margaret, the Maid of Norway, to be fetched from the north. Uprooted from home, the motherless girl took ill on the voyage and died in Orkney.

There were now a wide range of competing claims to the Scottish crown, mainly indirect descendants of the first Queen Margaret, but including one bid from descendants of Malcolm's family. These competitors represented four of Scotland's powerful aristocratic families – Bruce, Balliol, Comyn and de Soules. Civil war and anarchy threatened.

Under extreme pressure, the Guardians called in the neighbouring monarch, Edward I of England, to assist. In retrospect, given

England's previous claims to overlordship of Scotland and Edward's treatment of Wales, this seems like an extremely bad call. However, the Anglo-Norman royals of England were closely connected by marriage and landholdings with many of the Scottish nobles who had risen to power during the reigns of Malcolm and Margaret's successors. This was less the case with the traditional Celtic earldoms and Highland chiefs.

At a 1294 cross-border summit in Berwick, which Edward used to re-assert his 'overlordship', John Balliol was judged to have the best claim, and he succeeded to the throne. However, Edward treated him as a client ruler, while Balliol's subservience earned him the contemptuous soubriquet 'Toom Tabard' – Empty Jacket. Finally, even Balliol had absorbed enough humiliation and withdrew his allegiance to Edward in 1296. Soon to be named 'Hammer of the Scots', Edward promptly invaded, deposed Balliol, who went into exile, and seized Edinburgh Castle, removing Scotland's state papers to London.

While still pretending to be exercising traditional rights as 'overlord', England was now an occupying power, and Edward was intent on obliterating Scotland's identity as an independent country by force. There were two obstacles in Edward's path. Firstly, Scotland is geographically extensive with diverse regions and terrains. Garrisoning key centres such as Edinburgh, Stirling, Perth and Inverness gave an illusion of control, while leaving a long list of areas unsecured.

Secondly, though a nation of diverse regions and cultures, one common oppressor had the potential to unite Scotland in opposition, especially if that enemy was England. Edward's imperial ruthlessness became counter-productive. The gut reaction is well summed up by Abbot Bower, who ascribes these words to the first major leader of Scotland's resistance, William Wallace.

'Scotland so desolate! You are far too credulous of lying words, and not ready for the disaster which is on its way. If you were to agree with me, you would not so easily put your neck under a foreign yoke.'

Wallace then quotes a well-remembered saying of his uncle, which he values above all riches.

This is the truth I tell you,
Of all things freedom's most fine.
Never submit to live myself
In the bonds of slavery entwined.

The long, stormy passage ahead was to be fully charted by our now familiar chroniclers – Fordun, Wyntoun and, in particular, Walter Bower. But it was also celebrated in a raft of narrative poems, many of which have been lost or absorbed into the chronicles as secondary sources. Yet two big-hitter narrative poems have come down to us in their entirety – John Barbour's *The Brus,* and Blind Harry's *The Wallace* which will be discussed in the next chapter.

These epic poems transcend the chroniclers in terms of literary merit and embody a new flowering of Scotland's literary tradition. Though many further traumas lay in the future, the nation overcame the existential threat to its existence and that legacy was embedded in these narratives to which Scotland was to repeatedly return for inspiration through later struggles.

That said, *The Brus* and *The Wallace* are very different in style and approach, both from each other and from Bower's *Scotichronicon*. So while they were all connected with one national narrative, it is valuable to treat them as distinctive works in their own right. In this and the following chapter, literature becomes established as the work of individual writers, though Anonymous still has a role.

Though he did not compile his chronicle until the 1400s, Bower provides the main backstory for Scotland's crisis. Walter Bower is always a statesman and churchman in his work, passionately devoted to the national cause. Born and brought up in Haddington in East Lothian, the young Bower must have been acutely aware of the impact of English aggression over decades. Walter was a student at The University of St Andrews soon after its foundation in 1410 and became an Augustinian Canon, quickly appointed by the Pope as Abbot of Inchcolm. This was on account of his ability, as there is no evidence of any aristocratic connections.

From Inchcolm, close to Dunfermline and Edinburgh, Abbot Bower was well placed to take a full part in the councils and parliaments of state. He was also able to use the libraries at Dunfermline and St Andrews. Bower played a role in ransoming James I from England, and his subsequent reforming government. He was devastated by the young King's assassination in 1437.

Bower devoted much of his last years to literary composition, but could go no further than those bloody and tragic events. He closed his work with a eulogy of James and a poetic lament, and died soon afterwards. Bower wrote in Latin as the *lingua franca* of Europe, but he is lively and vivid. The *Scotichronicon* has been finely translated, and Abbot Walter deserves to be read. Here is his final poetic sign-off from Inchcolm, acknowledging his predecessor

John of Fordun, and re-affirming his core purpose through to the
last page.

> Be silent, breeze, my ship has reached the shore. Gladly I abandon
>   the seas
> and come to a halt, praise and glory to Christ.
> Here this work comes to an end and the author ceases to write
> the book which he is accustomed to call the *Scotichronicon*.
> This book covers the acts and awesome deeds
> Of kings, bishops, and likewise of the leading men of the people.
> Fordun has produced five books and the author eleven,
> which it will be clear to you make sixteen in all.
> So, reader, in return for their prayers we ask you to pray that
> both authors may be dwellers in the realm of the sky.
> **Christ! He is not a Scot who is not pleased with this book.**[1]

The Brus

We know much less about John Barbour, who wrote earlier than
Bower in the 1370s. *The Brus* is the earliest major work to be
written in Scots rather than Cymric, Latin or Gaelic. For much
of his life, Barbour was the Archdeacon of St Machar's Cathedral
in Aberdeen. This seems to have been a Court appointment in
recognition of diplomatic services at the Avignon papacy. Barbour
was often absent from Aberdeen, working at the Scottish Court.

Though there is an earlier record of Barbour being at Dunkeld
Cathedral, we do not know where he came from. However, the
prominence given in Barbour's work to Sir James Douglas suggests
that either he had some links to the Douglas lordships in southern

Scotland, or that he had access to detailed sources about the House of Douglas. Barbour's court connections, particularly in the reign of Robert II, are also reflected in a strand of the poem about Sir Walter Stewart, High Steward of Scotland. It was Stewart's marriage to Robert the Bruce's daughter Marjorie that began the line of royal Stewarts.

Overall, it is on his epic poem that we depend for our knowledge of this author. John Barbour champions the cause of Scottish independence as a background to his poem, but patriotism is not his primary focus. Also, though he acknowledges in a conventional way 'the grace of God', he is more interested in fate or destiny. Barbour's true subject is chivalry, and what constitutes chivalric behaviour. In this question, he enlists classical writers and French Romances to provide examples and comparisons. At times, these become a drag on the pace of Barbour's narrative drive over twenty books. However, his first readers would have appreciated some moral commentary, and contemporary readers can draw breath.

Describing Barbour as a poet of chivalry could, however, be misleading. The poet is not composing a *Chanson de Roland* in which a germ of historic happenings has grown into a powerful legendary fiction. As Barbour makes clear from the start, he is concerned with truth (suthfast) as well as storytelling.

> Storys to rede are delatibill (delightful)
> Suppos that they be nocht but fabyll.
> Then should storys that suthfast were,
> And that were said in guid manner,
> Have double pleasance in hearing.

> The first pleasance is the carping (telling),
> And the tother the suthfastness
> That schawis the thing richt as it was.

The poet's purpose, he continues, is to tell a 'suthfast' story, so that the valorous deeds of men 'that hardy was of heart and hand' will be remembered.

There is more realism than straight Romance in Barbour's epic. For him, 'chivalry' includes brutal conflict close-ups and cunning deceit, as well as exceptional courage. Also the author's 'delight' assumes some hard-nosed, sceptical tones, at points addressing his readers and even his characters with ironic taunts and sarcastic asides. To read Barbour as principally a historic source is a diversion from his outstanding qualities as a Scottish writer of the first rank. He also anticipates many later Scottish authors such as John Knox, who claim 'suthfastness' for their accounts, while deploying a literary persona all their own.

Barbour has a quartet of key 'chivalric' heroes in *The Brus*. They are, firstly, Robert the Bruce and his 'shadow' hero brother Sir Edward Bruce. Edward is flawed by his rashness and headlong personal decision making. Alongside the Bruces are Sir James Douglas and Sir Thomas Randolph, later Earl of Moray. Though Moray is Bruce's nephew, and of higher status, Barbour maximises the role of 'The Douglas' at every opportunity, placing Moray in his shadow. The structure of the poem revolves around these four, and plays out through constant interactions between the heroes and shadow heroes, and between the duos.

Chivalry is shown to be a product of character and action in combination. A prime example of this is when Edward Bruce 'rashly' agrees a truce with the English garrison at Stirling Castle. If not relieved by an English army within the year, they will surrender. As Robert the Bruce angrily points out, that is giving the military juggernaut of England a year to gather all its disproportionate resources. Edward's response is 'we shall fight, however many they be'. His elder brother relents.

> 'Brother, since so is gane
> That this thing is undertane,
> Schape we this thing manely,
> And all that luffis us tenderly,
> And the fredome of this countre,
> Purvey (equip) them at that time to be
> Bourne (ready) with all mycht that ever they
> So giff that our fayis (foes) assay
> To rescue Strivallane throu bataill,
> That we of purpos gar them faill.'

The originally unintended result is the Battle of Bannockburn through which, in Barbour's summing up, the wheel of fortune dramatically turns, placing Robert I of Scotland at the top, and Edward II of England at the foot.

Bannockburn is the poem's central set piece, staged over four books. Yet it is not the culmination of *The Brus*, which continues with events in Ireland, where the Bruces invade and Edward 'rashly' loses his life. Also in focus are the continuing struggles in southern Scotland, where Berwick is captured and besieged and the two bordering nations invade each other. This field of action gives Thomas Randolph, Earl of Moray, his chance to shine.

The first nine books of *The Brus* are a gripping account of the competition for the Scottish crown, Edward I's occupation, and the long, desperate resistance waged by Robert the Bruce, effectively as an outlaw in his own kingdom. In Barbour's version, this includes a sequence of incidents in which Bruce personally evades death, capture and assassination, demonstrating strength, combat skills, cunning and an uncanny ability to read character and act on his instincts. Bruce also displays a close knowledge of the terrain and how to use 'rough bounds' to military advantage.

All of this collectively ensures Bruce's survival as King of Scots, despite a ruthless English manhunt, aided and abetted by supporters of John Comyn, whom Bruce had murdered, as well as Scots who sided with the occupiers out of self-interest. On one occasion in Galloway, Bruce keeps watch alone at night while his small band rests on the other side of a river. A substantial force of horsemen approach, but Bruce holds the narrow path single handed, killing 14 assailants, until his men arrive.

On another occasion, Bruce rises early to relieve himself in a wood. Three assassins are waiting, but he manages to outwit them in close combat and kill all three in turn. If these events are exaggerated, it is detailed and convincing exaggeration. They are surely 'suthfast'. The common thread in these and many other events is Bruce's willingness to lead from the front with violent and effective action.

The struggle is bitter and deadly. Bruce's immediate family members are killed or imprisoned. Scots 'rebels' are drawn and quartered. Homes are raided and burned, with local people raped and murdered. In close combat, limbs are severed, head split to the shoulder and brains spilt. An early clash between Bruce and the MacDougalls of Lorne, who supported the English side, illustrates Barbour's blow-by-blow focus.

> Thai abaid (waited) till that he was
> Entryt in ane narrow place
> Betwixt a loch-sid and a bra (brae)
> That was sa strait (narrow) I underta
> That he mycht nocht weill turn in his steed.
> Then with a will till him thai yede (went)
> And ane him by the bridill hynt (seized),
> But he raucht till him sic a dynt (dunt)
> That arm and schuldyr flaw (flew) from him.

Attacker number two gets his hand caught in Bruce's stirrup and is dragged along, but number three climbs above the King in the narrow pass, posing an immediate threat. Bruce rises in his stirrups to deliver a mighty sword stroke that cleaves the enemy's head in two. This manoeuvre was to be repeated before Bannockburn when, riding only a small pony, Bruce stood in his stirrups to kill a fully armoured and mounted English knight.

An interesting feature of the guerrilla war is Bruce's encounters with ordinary people, enemies and friends. This is not part of Barbour's chivalric design which is focussed on those of noble birth and status. He speaks dismissively of 'the common sort' and even 'the rabble', only acknowledging their part, as at Bannockburn, when absolutely necessary. But of necessity, Bruce has to survive amongst his people and in the 'suthfast' spirit, Barbour describes these encounters, along with Bruce's respect for his supporters regardless of status.

Further, violence and hatred are not the preserve of Barbour's 'lower orders' in *The Brus*. These poisons reach the highest levels of the medieval hierarchy in this brutal conflict. Edward I dies in Cumbria on his way north to crush the treacherous Bruce. His last act is to deal with highborn Scots captives, who had been defending Bruce's wife and sister at Kildrummy Castle. They had surrendered and were entitled to imprisonment and ransom, according to the code of honour. Instead, a sickly, snarling Edward ordered 'hangis and drawys'. Barbour points out the irony that someone soon to be in the place of judgement, subject to divine mercy, should show no mercy himself. For once the churchman in Barbour comes to the fore.

Gradually Bruce wins local control area by area, along with the confidence of his subjugated people. This slow grind is then capped by the King's against-the-odds victory over a full English army at Loudoun Hill in Ayrshire. Throughout these grim years, Bruce displays an iron will and endurance. After finally succumbing to illness and exhaustion at Inverurie, he insists on leading the ravaging of the Comyns' Buchan heartland from a litter.

Other turning points include Sir James Douglas taking his own castle at Douglas in Lanarkshire, followed by Roxburgh Castle on the English border. Then comes Randolph's daring re-capture of Edinburgh Castle, the kingdom's principal stronghold. A local man, William Francis, who had once visited his lover in the town from the castle garrison by night, showed Randolph how the Rock could be scaled. The actual castle wall then had to be climbed with a 12-foot ladder. Randolph himself led the ascent, and the vulnerable group had to cling to an exposed ledge in the darkness, waiting to raise the ladder between sentries. Three men got over and then held the rampart for the others. With only 30 men in total but surprise on their side, the garrison was defeated and the premier fortress restored to its king. The propaganda value was as great as the strategic advantage.

Barbour's delight brims over when such a heavily outnumbered group turns the tables through bold, warlike leadership from the front. Their names should endure far beyond their own time, exults the author.

> For their worschip (valour) and their bounté (skill)
> Be lestand (lasting) aye forth in loving,
> Whar he that is of hevynnis king
> Bring them up till hevynnis blis
> Whar allwayis lestand loving is.

These lines exude the poet's enthusiasm for hardihood, rather than a churchman's considered view on rewards in the afterlife!

A similar qualification can be applied to Barbour's often quoted lines on freedom.

> A! Fredome is a noble thing
> Fredome mays (lets) man to haiff liking.
> Fredome all solace to man giffis,
> He levys at es (ease) that frely levys.
> A noble hart may haiff nane es
> Na ellys nocht that may him ples
> Gyff fredome failyhe, for fre liking
> Is yharnt (desired) oer all other thing.
> Na he that ay has levyt fre

> May nocht knaw weill the propyrté
> The angyr na the wrechyt dome
> That is couplt to foule thyrldome,
> Bot gyff he had assayit it.
> Than all perquer (perfect) he suld it wyt (know),
> And suld think fredome mar to prys
> Than all the gold in warld that is.

This is the theory, or at least the rhetoric, but the night before Bannockburn, in Barbour's account, Bruce delivers a more grounded assessment of what the Scots are fighting for. Firstly, they are in the right, defending their nation against an unjust oppressor. Secondly, the invaders have brought great riches which will fall to the Scots as booty if they win. Thirdly, the home side are fighting for their lives, and those of their wives and children – the would-be conquerors will show no mercy.

It is a well-judged speech combining some principles with the immediate balance between peril and gain. Again, the impression is of a 'suthfast' account. Another Scottish poet, Robert Burns, was to use this speech as the basis of his song 'Scots Wha Hae' in the context of British oppression after the French Revolution.

John Barbour looks back to the high middle ages and forward to late medieval humanism. His last salute to Bruce is the King's desire that his heart will go on crusade, even though his shattered body can no longer undertake the journey. The Douglas/Randolph dichotomy holds to the last, as Sir James is chosen to take the Bruce's heart to the Holy Land, while Moray becomes Regent after King Robert's death. Douglas loses his life on this quest.

Barbour's command of structure also shows in other roundings up. Descendants of the losing competitors of 1294 – de Soules and Comyn – conspire to overthrow the ailing king, and are executed for their efforts. More positively, a treaty of peace with England is finally agreed and the young King Edward III's sister Joan is married to Bruce's son, Prince David.

As mentioned, Barbour also strikes a courtier's note when he laments the death of Sir Walter Stewart and references the long reigns of the first two Stewart Kings, David II and Robert II, respectively the son and nephew of Robert the Bruce.

> God grant that thai that Comyn ar
> Of his offspring manteyne the land
> And hald the folk weill to warand (security)
> And manteyne rycht and leawté (loyalty)
> Als wele as in his tyme did he.

This relationship between poetry and the politics of the Stewart court was to be a central plank of literary endeavour in Scotland for centuries to come.

In the immediate context, however, the most striking evidence of Barbour's distinctive angle is his failure to even mention William Wallace. The poet of chivalry, like the chroniclers, knew of Wallace's historic role in the national story, but Barbour is not providing a historic account of the English wars. Moreover his focus is on the aristocratic caste, and he may not have welcomed the perspective, later expounded by Bower, that it was Wallace who had inspired Bruce to join the patriotic struggle.

Though Walter Bower accorded Wallace his place in history and legend, it was left to Blind Harry the minstrel, a century after Barbour, to give Wallace his own master narrative. But *The Wallace* emerged in a different Scotland and a much enlarged literary environment. John Barbour should be remembered as a pioneering Scots writer on a large canvas of his own making.

FOUR

The 15th Century: Poetry and Song

The First Renaissance

THE 15TH AND 16th centuries produced a literary flourishing in Scotland which became an acknowledged bedrock of excellence through the centuries. Yet at the time it was hardly noticed, until things were on the wane.

That may partly have been down to continuing political and military struggles. One after another the Stewart kings – successive Jameses – died young by assassination, accident or illness. Though external foes, notably England, played their part, instability was often caused by conflict between the royal government and the aristocratic magnates and clan chiefs, who ruled swathes of Scotland like monarchs and commanded their own military muscle. These over-mighty lords recognised the importance of the nation and its powers, but they wanted their own hands moving the levers whenever possible.

Perhaps more significantly, the poetic renaissance was not especially recognised because it formed part of wider ongoing cultural change. This is often ascribed to 'Humanism', which refers to the influence of Greek and Latin literature (the Classics), but also to an expanding sense of what it means to be human. This involved growing interests in geography, art, trade, languages, numbers, astronomy and astrology, plants and medicine, women's lives, sexuality, magic and folklore, in addition to inherited preoccupations with religion, fate, death and war. Lives of the blessed Saint Margaret had little to say about trade or sexual relations, while poets like Barbour, as we have seen, had their own limited sense of what made for a good life.

All of these developments became clearer in retrospect when, in 1507–8, Chepman and Myllar started Scotland's first printing press in Edinburgh with the active support of James IV. Choices were then made about what to print, and a poetic tradition began to take shape. Longer works such as Harry's *The Wallace* found a larger audience.

Later in the 16th century when instability and war, exacerbated by religious conflict, shook Scotland to its core, some people began to collect and anthologise. The realisation grew that there had been a golden age, a Renaissance, and that it was now under threat. These collectors included the venerable courtier Sir Richard Maitland, who summed up the retrospective mood in gloomy terms.

> Whair is the blythnes that has been
> Baith in burgh and landwart seen
> Among lordis and ladyis schein (beautiful)
> Daunsing, singing, game and play?
> But now I wait (know) not what they mein,
> All merriness is worne away.

In 1568, Edinburgh merchant George Bannatyne was confined for three months by the threat of plague, and assembled a significant manuscript of Scots poetry. His surviving papers suggest an earlier draft plan, perhaps to coincide with the wedding of Mary Queen of Scots and Lord Darnley in 1565. For a moment, it seemed as if a new era of peace and prosperity might be inaugurated. But by 1568 Darnley had been assassinated and Mary overthrown, so the need to retain what might be lost was more pressing. Some 'Protestant' edits for the new regime were also in order. Sadly, Bannatyne's great work was not published till centuries later, yet he did preserve and to some extent define the great tradition.

Three Poet Kings

What has been called Scotland's 'aureate', or golden age, conveniently begins with the poetic monarch James I who reigned from 1406 to 1437. He consciously brought new English and European influences to Scotland, not least through the work of the poet Geoffrey Chaucer. Matters poetic reach a peak with James IV between 1488 and 1513. He vigorously projected Renaissance kingship with its accompanying military ambition and cultural glamour. The golden age of literature ends with another poet king, James VI, between 1567 and 1625. His self-conscious efforts to revive the poetic tradition became known as the 'Castalian Band', but actually presaged decline, before James himself was transposed from Edinburgh to London through the Union of the Crowns in 1603.

James I inaugurates the new poetry in Scotland with his own accomplished solo work *The Kingis Quair*. This long poem is a vision of love, expressed with formal poise and lyric intensity. The *Quair* or Book appears to directly narrate the king's own experience during his 18-year detention in England. There he sees and falls in love with Princess Joan of England, whom he marries after returning to Scotland aged 24.

James' capture, aged six, was not primarily down to English perfidy but to internecine dynastic strife in Scotland which led to the young heir being sent to France for safety. He was not imprisoned but under house arrest in royal palaces, where he enjoyed an English education which included the works of the poet Geoffrey Chaucer who had died in 1400.

The Kingis Quair opens like a medieval dream vision, yet from the start there is a convincing immediacy of experience. Like Barbour, the young poet injects fresh realism into the medieval forms, evoking both the beauty of the garden below his tower and the emotions in looking on from his confinement.

> Bewailing in my chamber thus allone,
> Despeired of all joye and remedye,
> For-tirit of my thoght and wo begone,
> And to the wyndow gan I walk in hy
> To see the warld and folk that went forby;
> As for the tyme, though I of mirthis food
> Myght have no more, to luke it did me gude.
>
> Now was there maid fast by the touris wall
> A gardyn fair, and in the corneris set
> Ane herber grene with wandis long and small
> Railit about; and so with trees set
> Was all the place, and hawthorn hedgis knet,
>
> ....
>
> And on the small grene twistis sat
> The lytill suete nyghtingale and song
> So loud and clere the hymnis consecret
> Of lufis use, now soft, now lowd among,

> That all the gardyng and the wallis rong
> Ryght of thair song and of the copill (stanza) next
> Of thair swete harmony; and lo the text:
> 'Worschippe, ye that loveris bene, this May,
> For of your blisse the kalendis ar begonne,
> And sing with us, "Away, winter, away!
> Cum, somer, cum, the suete sesoun and sonne!"
> Awake, for schame! that have your hevynnis wonne,
> And amorously lift up your hedis all:
> Thank Lufe that list you to his merci call.'

The birds are singing their praises of love, but what is this 'love'? And why can the birds sing of it when he is cut off and alone? The answer to these questions comes more swiftly than might have been expected.

> And therwith kest I doun myn eye again,
> Quhare as I saw, walking under the tour,
> Full secretly new cummyn hir to playne (play),
> The fairest or the freschest yong floure
> That ever I sawe, me thoght, before that houre;
> For which suddayn abate anon astert
> The blude of all my body to my hert.
>
> And though I stude abaisit tho a lyte (little)
> No wonder was, for why my wittis all
> Were so overcom with plesance and delyte,
> Onely through letting of myn eyen fall,
> That suddaynly my hert became hir thrall

> Forever, of free wyll; for of menace
> There was no tokyn in hir swete face.

Setting and occasion conjoin in a persuasive account of falling in love at first sight. The experience is natural, personal and to some degree cosmic. Music connects those three through bird-song, poetic metre and the music of the spheres. Every so often a stanza is marked 'cantus' – to be sung – and the poem itself concludes as a hymn of praise to the divine force of love.

> Blissit mot (may) be the goddis all,
> So fair that glateren (glitter) in the firmament!
> And blissit be thare myght celestiall
> That have convoyit hale with one assent
> My lufe, and to so glade a consequent!
> And thankit be Fortunys axiltree
> And whele, that thus so wele has whirlit me!

A similar alignment of human passion with the green sap of May appears in 'Tayis Bank', another important love poem, which is associated with James IV. But here the heavenly dimension is omitted in favour of a more earthly lust.

> When Tayis bank was blumyt brycht,
> With blosumes brycht and braid (wide),
> By that river that ran doun rycht
> Under the ryss I red (boughs I rode);
> The merle (blackbird) melit (mixed notes) with all her mycht
> And mirth in mornying maid,

Throw solace, sound, and semely sicht,
Alsuth (at once) a sang I said.

Undir that bank, whair bliss had bene,
I bownit me (got ready) to abyde;
Ane holene (holly), hevinly hewit grene,
Rycht heyndly (graciously) did me hyd;
The sone schyne our the schawis schene (lovely groves)
Full semely me besyde;
In bed of blumes bricht besene (arrayed)
A sleip couth (did) me ourslyd.

About all blumet was my bour
With blosumes broun and blue,
Oerfret with mony fair fresch flour,
Helsum of hevinly hue;
With shakeris of the schene dew schowr
Schynnyng my curtenis schew,
Arrayit with a rich vardour
Of natouris werkis new.

Beside the running river and the blossomed banks, the poet, officially anonymous, sees a 'lusum' or lovesome one as fair as any under the firmament of heaven.

Scho wes the lustiest on live,
Allone lent on a land,
And fairest figuor, by sic syve (seven times),

> That evir in firth I fand,
> Her comely cullour to discryve
> I dar nocht tak on hand;
> Moir womanly borne of a wyfe
> Wes never, I dar warrand.

The woman in question is no dream vision, but Margaret Drummond of Stobhall 'where Tay ran doun with streamis stout / full strecht under Stobschaw.' She was James IV's mistress, who died of poison with her three sisters nine months before James married Princess Margaret of England. Rumour suggested that the poisoning was a deliberate act by the pro-English faction at court to prevent the king marrying his lover. Rumour also ascribed the poem to James himself. Whether this is true or not, the poem is inspired by James' love for Margaret Drummond.

'Anonymous' later gave way to court poet William Dunbar who penned 'The Thrissil and the Rose', a very official ode on James' marriage to Princess Margaret. But 'Tayis Bank' remains a strong reminder that Scotland's first poetic renaissance was not a subset of Chaucerian English. Many different streams flowed into the Scottish current, including Anonymous. Also active, though at one remove from the Stewart court, was the Gaelic tradition, where music played a full part in performing poetry as a public art. Women's voices are heard directly in Gaelic tradition as in this love poem by Ní Mheic Cailéin, wife of Colin first Earl of Argyll.

> Alas for him whose sickness is love,
> For what cause soever I should say it;
> Hard it is to be free of it;

Sad is the plight in which I am myself.
Is mairg dá ngalar an grádh,
Gé bé fáth n-abrainn é;
Deacair sgaractainn ré pháirt;
Truagh an cás i bhfeilim féin.

Love transforms into searing lament in the raw verses of 'Griogal Cridhe', a lament on the death of Griogair MacGregor of Glenstrae.

Early on Lammas morning
I was sporting with my love:
Before midday came
My heart was broken.

Ochain, ochain, ochain uiridh
Sore is my heart, my dear.
Ochain, ochain, ochain uiridh
Your father cannot hear our cry.

A curse on nobles and kinsfolk
Who have torn me so with pain,
Who came without warning upon my love
And by treachery made him captive.

They placed his head on a block of oak,
And spilt his blood on the ground;
Had I only held a cup then
I would have drunk my fill.

Moch madainn air latha Lùnasd'
Bha mi sùgradh mar ri m' ghràdh,
Ach mun tàinig meadhon latha
Bha mo chridhe air a chràdh.

Ochain, ochain, ochain uiridh
Is goirt mo chridhe, a laoigh,
Ochain, ochain, ochain uiridh
Cha chluinn t' athair ar caoidh.

Mallachd aig maithibh is aig càirdean
Rinn mo chràdh air an-dòigh,
Thàinig gun fhios air mo ghràdh-sa
Is a thug fo smachd e le foill.

Chuir iad a cheann air ploc daraich,
Is dhòirt iad fhuil mu làr:
Nam biodh agam-sa an sin cupan,
Dh' òlainn dith mo shàth.

This poem is ascribed by tradition to Marion Campbell, whose father had ordered Griogair's killing. The intensity of these love poems raises everyone involved to a unique status, defined by clan descent and pure passion.

As regards kingly poets, James VI, last of the three, was not in the front rank of love poetry. In his *Amatoria*, James argues for and against praising his new queen, Anne of Denmark. He employs deflating imagery, like blood boiling as if in a bedpan. Women, he reckons, waver like a weathercock and 'as sea that still can never be.' More peevish perhaps than passionate?

James VI was, however, tutored by a great poet of the day, George Buchanan. He set out rules for writing poetry in Scots and was a proactive patron of other poets, including Alexander Montgomerie, whose 'Cherrie and the Slae' is a finely wrought religious allegory. Hailing from Ayrshire, Montgomerie was comfortable with Scots, Gaelic and English. But as a courtier in Edinburgh and a Roman Catholic, he got into political troubles and was banished. James' own literary importance grew as Shakespeare's patron and commissioner of the Authorised Version of the Bible. His consort, Anne, unsurprisingly turned to other poets such as Ben Jonson rather than depend on James. We will return to this exceptional royal couple when we consider the later arts of theatre.

Robert Henryson

The celebration of nature in 15th-century poetry was accompanied by a new strand of urban awareness. The Scottish burghs, especially Edinburgh, were growing and producing a wider readership through education. The urban note is intimate and assured in the work of Robert Henryson who, after academic training in Glasgow and perhaps on the continent, settled as a schoolmaster in Dunfermline. There he found time to write sophisticated European poetry such as his skilfully fashioned version of 'Orpheus and Eurydice', but also to produce in his *Fables* poems for a more popular readership, including those who would have heard rather than read the texts.

Henryson's Morall *Fabillis* are a genial Scots expansion of Aesop's Greek fables, so the schoolmaster is not lost, but the Scots tales are witty, playful and wise. They speak to a wide social base rather than to a castle or court. The tale of 'The Town Mouse and the Country Mouse', for example, seems made for Dunfermline with its busy town amidst the farmland and countryside of Fife. In 'The Sheep and the Dog', a wolf poses fraudulently as a judge, tapping into people's knowledge of the burgh and church courts with all the ups and downs of their legal process.

> For by the use and cours (legal custom) and common
>   style,
> On this manner made his citatioun:
> 'I, maister wolf, partless of fraud and gyle,
> Under the painis of hie suspensioun,
> Of grit cursing, and interdictioun,
> Sir Scheip, I charge thee straitly to compeir,
> And answer to a dog before me here.'

In 'The Cock and the Jasp', the interplay is between the cockerel on his urban dung heap and a slatternly woman who carelessly sweeps out the jasp or jewel, because she was in a rush to join the street life bustle and gossip.

Henryson proves himself master of his chosen form, which aims to highlight human folly with sweet rhetoric 'richt plesand' to the ear. And Henryson has an acute musical sense with a keen interest in metrical forms and harmonies. But this is deployed in service of a broader strategy representing people as animals, so disarming and yet also reinforcing his critique. The results continue to be insightful and delightful. Henryson seems to have continued to produce fables through his working life, perhaps using them as a kind of recreation between more demanding works.

The atmosphere of Robert Henryson's finest narrative poem, *The Testament of Cresseid,* is very different.

> Ane doolie (sad) sessoun to ane cairfull dyte (style)
> Suld correspond, and be equivalent.
> Richt sa it was when I began to wryte
> This tragedie, the wedder richt fervent
> When Aries in middis of the Lent
> Schouris of haill gart fra the north discend.

The tone is intimate and, despite the weather, Henryson sees Venus rising in the west between showers. Love is on the poet's mind, experienced as youthful fire but now as a failing force in old age.

> I mend the fyre and beikit (happed) me about
> Than tuik ane drink my spreitis to comfort
> And armit me weill fra the cauld thairout
> To cut the winter nicht and mak it schort.
> I tuik ane quair and left all uther sport.
> Writtin be worthie Chaucer glorious
> Of fair Creisseid, and worthie Troylus.

Henryson is tackling a known tale from the classical world – a Trojan wartime love story. He is drawing on Chaucer's version which in turn is based on Boccaccio's Italian rendering. However, this poet's focus is not, like previous versions, on Troilus but on Cresseid. What was her fate after she had lost Troilus and also been rejected by her own side in the Greek camp?

Cresseid feels betrayed by both sides due to her father's ambivalent politics. Yet she also feels betrayed by the goddess of love to whom she had surrendered. Venus' appearance brings her no comfort.

> Venus was thair present, that goddess
> Hir sonnis quarrell for to defend and mak
> Hir awin complaint, cled in ane nyce array,
> The ane half grene, the uther half sabill blak
> Whyte hair as gold kemmit and sched abak.
> Bot in hir face semit greit variance,
> Whyles perfyte treuth, and whyles inconstance.
> ....
> In taikning (as a token) that all fleschelie paramour
> Whilk Venus hes in reull and gouernance,
> Is sum tyme sweit, sum tyme bitter and sour
> Richt unstabill, and full of variance
> Mingit with cairfull joy and fals plesance,
> Now hait, now cauld, now blyth, now full of wo
> Now grene as leif, now widderit and ago (gone).

Cresseid falls ill with leprosy, considered in medieval times as a disease of promiscuity. She becomes an indigent beggar with a warning clapper – unclean, unclean. Henryson articulates her suffering with compassion and empathy. The climax of his narrative comes when Troilus, now commander of the Trojan army, encounters the lazarous Cresseid by the roadside. Despite her blighted body, he recognises her eyes.

> Than upon him scho kest up baith hir een,
> And with ane blenk it come into his thocht,

That he sumtime hir face befoir had seen.
Bot scho was in sic plye (such a state) he knew hir nocht,
Yit than hir luik into his mynd it brocht
The sweit visage and amorous blenking
Of fair Cresseid sumtyme his awin darling.

Troilus gives the beggar a belt of gold and jewels, but then departs. Then Cresseid realises that the generous knight was her own Troilus and bitterly regrets being swayed by her father to leave him. She writes a last testament – 'O fals Cresseid and trew knicht Troilus'. She realises that the instability of love needs human faithfulness if the promise of love is to be fulfilled.

Cresseid dies, but her grave is tended by Troilus for he too has been carried back in time and inwardly transformed by the roadside encounter.

Ane spark of lufe then till his hart culd spring,
And kendlit all his bodie in ane fyre.
With hait fevir ane sweit and trimbling
Him tuik, whill he was reddie to expyre.
To beir his scheild, his breist began to tyre
Within ane whyle he changit mony hew,
And nevertheles not ane uther knew.

In this subtle extension of the inherited tale, Henryson deepens the drama by adding his profound understanding of Christian love into the classical form. This is not achieved through preaching but by persuasively switching perspective to Cresseid's experiences and emotions, before returning to Troilus. This is a humanist and humane achievement, combining insight with skilful story-telling. Without fireworks, but with characteristic modesty and understatement, the schoolmaster of Dunfermline proves himself a world-class poet.

William Dunbar

Contrast could not be greater than between the home-loving poet of Dunfermline and William Dunbar, the restless court poet and priest in Edinburgh. The multifaceted Dunbar exhibits a modern consciousness combined with virtuoso technique which made this writer a favourite among later poets, including Robert Burns in the 18th and Hugh MacDiarmid in the 20th centuries.

Dunbar frequently contradicts himself, mocking religion in one poem and embodying sincere devotion in another. Among his longer works, 'The Goldyn Targe' is an allegory of love in the high style, while 'The Twa Mariit Wemen and the Wedo' is a no-holds-barred scabrous conversation between three women about their sex lives. Yet, though Dunbar's tone is often satiric, he generates lucent praises of the Virgin Mary and produced this unusually plain and sincere reckoning of men's dependence on women.

> Now of wemen this I say, for me,
> Of earthly things nane may better be.
> They should hauf wirschip and grit honouring
> Of men, aboif all uther earthly thing.

Perhaps the common thread in William Dunbar is a melancholy

sense of changefulness and disappointment, which he tries to keep at bay through the technical fireworks of his poetry.

> What is this lyfe bot ane straucht way to deid,
> Whilk hes a tyme to pas and nane to dwell,
> A sliding wheill is lent to seek remeid,
> A free choice gevin to paradice or hell,
> A prey to deid, whome vane is to repell,
> A schort torment for infineit glaidnes,
> Als schort ane joy for lestand hevynes.

Dunbar's melancholy sinks at times into downright depression, with repeated complaints that he has no office, role or reward for his efforts. He might be a knackered old horse, he says, turned out to die at Christmas to save a winter's feeding.

In Dunbar's case, we have to take the poetry as the person. Taken as a whole, William Dunbar's work is dazzling in its technical and linguistic range – a revelation of Edinburgh's first golden age of poetry. At the aureate end, he is close to Latin as in this 'Hymn to the Virgin'.

> Hale, sterne superne, hale, in eterne
> In Goddis sicht to schyne;
> Lucerne in derne (darkness) for to discerne
> Be glory and grace divine […]
> Ave Maria, gratia plena.

For official court poems, Dunbar was ready with a high register. But he could also produce unglossable stanzas from a flyting or exchange of abuse between poets, in this case Walter Kennedy and Dunbar. Judge, demands Dunbar, implicating us in the argument, who got the worst of it here.

> Iersche brybour baird, wyle beggar with thy brattis,
> Cuntbittin crawdoun, Kennedy, coward of kynd,
> Evill farit and dryit, as Dansmen on the rattis,
> Lyk as the gleddis had on thy gulesnowt dynd,
> Mismaid monstour, ilk mone out of thy mynd,
> Renunce, rebald, thy rymyng, thow bot ravis.
> Thy trechour tung hes tane ane Heland strynd,
> Ane Lawland ares wald mak a bettir noyis.

Such exchanges did not preclude poets continuing as friends – the point was to excel in invention, even if the main source was the urban gutters. Ironically, Dunbar also berated Edinburgh for its filthy streets!

Between these highs and lows, Dunbar could deliver personal shafts and social satire in calculated measure.

> My heid did yake yester nicht,
> Theis day to mak that I na micht.
> So sair the magryne does me menyie (afflict),
> Persing my brow as ony ganyie (arrow),
> That scant I luik may on the licht.

Or in more limber mood:

> Then cam in Dunbar the makar (poet);

On all the flair their was none frackar (more agile),
And their he dancet the dirrye dantoun (dance
imitating sexual intercourse)
He hoppet lik a pillie wanton (randy lecher).

Roll on Luther and Calvin! Yet Dunbar could also lambast others
for disorderly conduct, as in his 'Merchantis of Renown'.

Why will ye, merchantis of renoun,
Let Edinburgh, your nobill toun,
For laik of reformatioun
The commone proffeitt tyne (lose), and fame?
Think ye not schame,
That onie uther regioun,
Sall with dishonour hurt your name?

May nane pas throw your principall gaittis,
For stink of haddockis and of scaittis,
For cryis of carlingis (old biddies) and debaittis,
For feusum (foul) flyttingis of defame.
Think ye not schame,
Befoir strangeris of all estaitis,
That sic dishonour hurt your name?

Your Stinkand Styll, that standis dirk (dark),
Haldis the lycht fra your parroche kirk;
Your forestairis makis your housis mirk,
Lyk na cuntray bot here at hame.
Think ye not schame,

> Sa litill polesie to work,
> In hurt and sklander of your name?

Another notable victim of Dunbar's satire is John Damian, whom James IV made Abbot of Tongland in recognition of his contributions to Renaissance science and invention. Given Dunbar's own lack of preferment, this was a red rag to the poetic bull, further incited by the Abbot's claim that he could fashion wings and fly. To Dunbar's glee the attempt was a flop, and Dunbar heaped on the abuse accusing Damian of being a fraud, a son of Satan and a murderous doctor or 'homicide of leechcraft'.

Yet William Dunbar could also strike a sonorous, collective chord, as in the poem that develops into a 'Lament for the Makars', 'who plays thir pageant syne (then) goes to grief'.

> I that in heill wes and gladnes,
> Am trublit now with gret seiknes,
> And feblit with infermite;
> *Timor mortis conturbat me.* (Fear of death gives me distress)
> Our plesance heir is all vane glory,
> This fals warld is bot transitory,
> The flesche is brukle (frail), the Fend is slee;
> *Timor mortis conturbat me.*

Dunbar's catalogue of lost poets has become a prime source for the range of Scotland's 15th-century poetic renaissance, as for many of the names we have no surviving works.

Despite his satires on false religion, Dunbar's ear is well attuned to the deeper grounds of religious faith, as in this fine Easter poem.

> Done is a battle on the dragon black,
> Our champion Christ confoundit has his force;
> The yettis (gates) of hell are broken with a crack,
> The sign triumphal raisit is of the cross,
> The devillis trymmillis with hiddous voce,
> The saulis are borrowit (redeemed) and to the bliss can go,
> Christ with his bloud our ransomis dois indoce (confirm):
> *Surrexit Dominus de sepulchro.* (The Lord is risen from
> the tomb)
>
> Dungin (beaten) is the deidly dragon Lucifer,
> The cruwall serpent with the mortal stang;
> The auld kene (fierce) tiger, with his teeth on char (bared),
> Whilk in a wait has lyen for us so lang,
> Thinking to grip us in his clawis strang;
> The merciful Lord wald nocht that it were so,
> He made him for to failye of that fang.
> *Surrexit Dominus de sepulchro.*

There is always something to surprise and challenge in Dunbar. The individual is hard to nail down, but the poetry never fails to intrigue.

Arts of Narrative

Alongside literary innovation, the 15th and 16th centuries also sustained some older traditions. Epic and Romance themes, for example, continued in sung ballads, whose origins in oral culture can no longer be exactly pinpointed. Warlike episodes featured, such as the 14th-century Battle of Otterburn or the 15th-century clash at Harlaw between Highland and Lowland. These ballads continue to be sung. Equally persistent were the haunting dramatic and supernatural ballads focused on encounters of mystery, passion and sometimes violence. Again, many of these, including 'My Son David', 'Lord Randal', 'Tam Lin' and 'Thomas the Rhymer' were recorded direct from continuing oral traditions, and are still sung.

The narrative art of these poems is to seize the attention of the listener, and not let go till the tale has been played out, and received into the consciousness of the audience. This 'Ancient Mariner' technique, as exemplified by Coleridge, is well understood by tradition-bearers who talk of 'giving' the song or the story.

A ballad may begin in the midst of the drama.

> 'O what's the blood that's on your sword,
> My son David, O son David?
> What's that blood it's on your sword?
> Come promise, tell me true.'

> 'O that's the blood of my grey mair,
> Hey lady mither, ho lady mither
> That's the blood of my grey mair
> Because it widnae rule by me.'

> 'O that blood it is ower clear
> My son David, O son David
> That blood it is ower clear
> Come promise, tell me true.'

Or setting an epic event in motion.

> It fell about the Lammas tide
> When the muir men win their hay,
> That doughty Douglas bound him to ride
> Into England to hunt a prey.

Perhaps with an eyewitness.

> 'As I cam in by Durisdeer
> An doun by Netherha
> There were fifty thousand Hielanmen
> A mairching tae Harlaw.'

Or deftly setting the scene for a passionate encounter.

> True Thomas lay on Huntlie bank
> A ferlie he spied wi his ee
> And there he saw a fair ladye
> Come riding doun by the Eildon Tree.

Blind Harry the minstrel sits between the poets and the oral tradition. He was paid according to the Court records, probably for entertaining James IV who employed storytellers, singers and musicians. Yet *The Wallace* is another epic Romance, similar in scale to Barbour's *The Brus*.

Little else is known about Harry. Is that his surname? Was he blind from birth or perhaps in later life? Had he seen military service, given his poem's martial content? Did he come from Stirlingshire and Kinross, or the Borders? Did he write *The Wallace* in opposition to James III's policy of alignment with England? The answer to all these questions is that we have no firm evidence. Harry might as well be 'Anonymous'.

Yet, the impact of Harry's poem from the 1480s on is not in doubt. *The Wallace* is a compelling heroic biography which subordinates historical accuracy to patriotic, emotional punch. It succeeded for a long time in becoming Scotland's most widely owned book after the Bible, gaining fresh momentum from the 18th-century translation by William Hamilton, and then the 20th-century film adaptation *Braveheart*, directed by Mel Gibson.

At all points, Harry makes William Wallace's story personal. The hero is not a remote chivalric aristocrat but from a family of lairds closely connected with the common folk. One uncle is a priest. Wallace's young life, like that of many others, is marred by the English occupation. Then it is nearly destroyed by the brutal murder of his young wife.

Wallace's mission becomes revenge, accompanied by a growing desire to restore Scotland's freedom. He is called to this purpose in a vision by the Virgin Mary herself, who paints the cross of St Andrew on his face in blue and white. By the end, like Christ, he sacrifices body and soul to the cause. In Harry's telling, Wallace, though defeated, inspires others, including Robert the Bruce, to take up the burden and win freedom – something that cannot be treated lightly or ever again surrendered.

> Wallace commaundit his host tharfor to byd;
> Hys ten he tuk, for to meit Bruce thai ryd.
> Sowthwest he past, whar at the tryst was set;

86

The Bruce full son and gud Wallace is met.
For loss off Graham, and als for propyr teyn
  (pure grief),
He grew in ire, when he the Bruce had seyn.
Thar salusyng (greeting) was bot boustous and thrawin
  (rough and angry).
'Rewis thow,' he said, 'thow art contrar thine awin?'
'Wallace,' said Bruce, 'rabut (rebuke) me now no mair;
'Myn awin dedis has bet me wondyr sair.'
When Wallace heard with Bruce that it stud swa (so),
On kneis he fell, fair contenans can him ma (show).
……………………………………………………..
Wallace him prayit; 'Cum fra yon Southeron king.'
The Bruce said; 'Nay, thar lattis (prevents) me a thing.
I am so boundyn with wytnes (testimony) to be leill
  (loyal),
For all Ingland I wald nocht fals my seall.
Bot off a thing, I hecht (vow) to God and thee,
That contrar Scottis again I sall nocht be;
In till a feild, with wapynnys that I bear,
In thy purpos I sall thee nevir der (harm).

A strong feature of *The Wallace*, in contrast to Barbour's *The Bruce*, is the important part played by women. They are often the backbone of Scotland's resistance. In addition to Wallace's wife and lovers and the Virgin Mary, Harry has his hero meet Queen Margaret of England, Edward's queen. She responds warmly to his courtesy and respect. William Wallace was to be knighted and become a Guardian of Scotland, yet as an honoured gentleman he never lost the common touch.

For Harry the cause justifies all. Scotland has been raped and despoiled and there must be redress. Wallace sets about that task in a full-on, bloodthirsty manner. This expresses Harry's strong anti-English feelings which are conveyed in denigrating language and outright violence. The only brutality from which Harry averts his, and our, gaze is the savage extended execution and then dismemberment of Wallace at Smithfield in London. Perhaps that is too much for the minstrel to stomach. Harry's explicit violence can be criticised on grounds of taste and morality, but given contemporary events in Ukraine, the Sudan and Gaza, his stance may be more realistic than we care to acknowledge.

It is not possible to adequately represent *The Wallace* through scattered quotations. The poem is more like a novel which needs to be read at pace from the rebellious start, through struggle and triumph to martyrdom. William Hamilton of Gilbertfield's translation is a good place for present-day readers to begin, though he edits out the Virgin Mary for his own more Protestant times.

Gavin Douglas

Unlike Robert Henryson, who appears to have been someone of modest background, Gavin Douglas, Dean of St Giles and later Bishop of Dunkeld, was an aristocratic Douglas and as ambitious in his worldly career as in his art.

Gavin Douglas produced two monumental poems. *The Palice of Honour*, written before his royal appointment to St Giles, is an elaborate, extended allegory on the true nature of courtly honour. It is laden with learned allusions to classical mythology and the

Bible. *The Palice* may have been partly a pitch for preferment since it aligns closely with the high Renaissance values of James IV's court.

Douglas' second major poem, a Scots translation of Virgil's Latin epic *The Aeneid*, is even more ambitious. Like Troilus and Cresseid, this was a familiar tale to educated readers, not least because the wanderings of Aeneas and his descendants had been chosen as an English foundation legend, and used to justify Edward I's takeover of Scotland. Douglas was cocking a snoot at England by making this first poetic translation into Scots. For avoidance of doubt, Douglas says in his prologue that an English prose version from the French, which had been published by William Caxton, had as much to do with *The Aeneid* as the Devil with St Augustine.

Soon Douglas was embroiled in his long, drawn-out task to render the master of Roman epic into literary Scots in between ecclesiastical and political affairs. At some point he decided to go a stage further by adding his own poetic prologue to each book of Virgil. The result is *The Eneados*, a two-decker masterwork in which the poet sets out his own creative and Scottish perspective before resuming the core translated narrative. The implication is clear – Scots literature claims its place alongside the classics.

This was a work of years, and the number of readers able to judge the project's all-round success may now be limited. While aiming to keep his language 'broad and plain', Douglas himself advises that his poem has to be read and savoured more than once to get the full meaning. This presumes that private readers will be poring over his rich text rather than listening to a public recitation.

Douglas also assumes a modest stance, giving the credit to 'maist reverend Virgil, of Latin poets prince / gem of ingyne and flood of eloquence'. His version is 'rude, vulgar verse' by comparison, yet his own ambition holds good, 'that thy fecund sentence mycht be sang / in our language as well as Latin tongue'.

Savour this intense extract – Dido's invective against the faithless, departing Aeneas, foreshadowing her own death.

> Nothir will I hald thee, nor thi wordis contrar:
> Pass on thy way, towart Itale thou fair;
> Seik throu the fludis with wyndis to that ryng.
> Forsuth, if reuthfull goddis may ony thing,
> Amid thi way, I traist, on rolkis blak
> Thou sal deir (injure) by thy treuth thou to me brak,
> And clepe (call) oft my richt name, Dido, Dido!
> With fyre infernale, in thine absens also
> I sal thee follow; and, fra the cauld ded
> Reif from my membris this saule, in every sted
> My ghost sal be present thee to aggrys:
> Thou salt, unworthy wyght, upon this wys,
> Be punyst weil; and tharof wald I heer;
> The fame tharof sal cum onto myne ear,
> Undir the erth, amang the schaddowis law (low).

And put beside that, an example of the evocative seasonal mood from Gavin Douglas' prologue to Book VII: sheltering by the fire, he sees Virgil's text sitting on his lectern and once more takes up his pen, echoing Henryson's wintry labours.

> The frosty regioun ringis (reigns) of the year,
> The tyme and season bittir, cauld, and paill,
> Tha schort days that clerkis clepe (call) brumail,

When brym (fierce) blastis of the northern airt
Oerwhelmit had Neptunus in his cart,
And all to schaik the leavis of the trees,
The rageand storm ourweltrand wally (rolling over
    stormy) seas;
Riveris ran reid on spait with wattir broune,
And burnys hurlys all thar bankis doune,
And landbrist (surf breaking) rumland rudely with sik
    beir (cries),
So lowd ne rumist (roared) wild lyoun or bear.
....
So bustously Boreas his bugill blew,
The deer full dern (hidden) doun in the dalis drew;
Small birdis, flokkand throu thik ronis (branches)
thrang,
In chirming and with cheping changit thar sang,
Sekand hidlis and hirnis (corners) thame to hyde
Fra feirfull thuddis of the tempestous tide.
....
And, as I bounit me to the fyre me by,
Baith up and down the hows I dyd aspy:
And seand Virgil on a lettron stand,
To write onone I hint (caught) a pen in hand,
Fortil perform the poet grave and sad.

If this is failure, what could possibly constitute success? Certainly,
Gavin Douglas' legacy is his poetry, since the Bishop's worldly
career ended sadly in London after James IV's calamitous defeat
at the Battle of Flodden in 1513.

Tailpiece

Before concluding the 15th century, it is worth acknowledging the vigorous humour that marks so many narrative poems from this period. Scottish literature abounds in every form on the spectrum from broad and bawdy to deprecating and ironic.

In addition to the named poets, the offerings of Anonymous include 'The Cokelbie Sow' – a rural farce; 'Rauf Coilyear' – a take-off of knightly Romance; 'The Friaris of Berwick' – a satire on the sexual antics of the Franciscans; and 'Christis Kirk on the Green' – a rowdy folk celebration of the Beltane or May Fair. Another, perhaps more accessible, example is 'The Wyfe of Auchtermuchty'.

After a hard day in the fields, the gudeman insists on sending his wife out to plough the next morning while he takes charge of domestic affairs with predictably disastrous and hilarious results. This poem only survives in the Bannatyne Manuscript.

> Then ben there cam' ane greedy sow,
> I trow he cunnd (gave) her little thank,
> For in she shot her mekle mou,
> And aye she winkit and aye she drank.
> He cleikit up (grabbed) ane crookit club,
> And thought to hit the sow ane rowt,
> The twa goslings the gled (hawk) had left,
> That straik dang baith their harns (brains) owt.
> ....
> Then he gaed to tak' up the bairns,
> Thought to have found them fair and clean,
> The first that he gat in his arms,

Was all bedirten to the een.
'The deil cut off her hands,' quoth he,
'That filled ye a' sae fou yestreen!'
He trail'd the foul sheets down the gait (road),
Thought to have washed them on ane stane;
The burn was risen great of spate,
Away frae him the sheets were taen.

Then up he gat on ane knowe-head,
On her to cry, on her to shout;
She heard him, as she heard him not,
But stoutly steerd the stots (oxen) about.
She drave the day unto the night,
She lowsd the pleugh, and syne cam hame;
She fand all wrang that should been right;
I trow (believe) the man thought right great shame.

'My office I forsake,' he declares abjectly, 'for all the dayis of my life.
For I and this house will never do weill.' It is a thorough vindication
of the capable gudewife, and a satisfying ending.

FIVE

16th Century: History and Drama

History Hector

AS THE 15TH century turned in to the 16th, history writers were lagging behind the achievement of Scotland's poets. Yet there was a lot of history happening. In 1488, James III had been overthrown and then assassinated at Sauchie. His son James IV, who was implicated in these events, succeeded to the throne and became the nation's pre-eminent Renaissance ruler. Then in 1513 he invaded England at the request of France and, refusing to retreat from the frontline, was slaughtered alongside the flower of Scotland's nobility on Flodden field.

The subsequent minority of James V was uneasy, as court factions competed for influence over the boy-king. At the same time, religious disputes spread across Europe, and the Church – still Scotland's backbone institution – was notably lacking in its earlier saintly qualities.

Against this background, chroniclers, unlike the poets, had not produced any new master narratives. Scotland's leading philosopher, John Mair or Major, had written a commentary in Latin on historical issues, but it was academic in style and also advocated a Union between England and Scotland, which had little appeal to Scottish readers. Yet Major's ideas about putting limitations on royal power were to bear fruit later, not least in the work of his students, who included John Knox and George Buchanan.

More immediate help was, however, at hand in the shape of Hector Boece – Boyce in Scots. A brilliant student at St Andrews and then Paris, where he became close friends with the European humanist Erasmus, this young Dundonian was lured in 1500 from Paris to Aberdeen University by its founder William Elphinstone, Bishop of Aberdeen and Chancellor of Scotland. There Boece embarked on writing history in a new humanist style, beginning with a dutiful account of Aberdeen's early Bishops, before proceeding to the national narrative.

Hector Boece writes in flowing Latin, which was admired across Europe, but his project really took fire at home when his work was freely translated into Scots, at James IV's request, by John Bellenden, a court official. The model for both writers was the Latin historian Livy, who had devised a master narrative for the Roman Empire rooted in its origins as a hardy, vigorous republic. Bellenden went on to also translate Livy into Scots, while Boece applied Livy's principles to Scotland.

The answer to present challenges, asserted Boece, was to re-apply the patriotic virtues which pre-dated the influence of 'Inglis maneris in our breistis.' The historian's sharpest critique was aimed at an aristocratic caste which was, in Boece's view, thirled to luxury and contention while presuming their entitlement to rule Scotland. The faith of a pioneering Christian kingdom should be rediscovered.

Yit I am nocht so disparit, but traistis, within schort time, that all corrupt maneris of our pepill sall be reparit to ane better fassoun: for nocht allanerly, in sindry partis of this realme, remainis yit the futsteppis of mony auld virtewis usit sum time amang our eldaris. But als risis every day new fervent devotioun, to the ornament of Cristin faith.

In this regard Boece picks up again where Abbot Bower had left off. Yet we are also hearing the voice of a Roman Catholic reformer, at the start of the 16th century, urging improvement in social manners and government. Conflicting visons of reform were to dominate the century ahead.

Boece has not found much favour with modern historians, who accuse him of putting style before accurate substance. In particular he is charged with inventing 40 extra Scottish kings, whose supposed portraits still decorate the Palace of Holyroodhouse. It is, however, possible that Hector may have been drawing on a lost source which he then embroidered.

What is indisputable is that Boece was a literary success in Latin and Bellenden's Scots. He has an authentic narrative gift and is always ready to fill any gaps with creative flair. One glowing or, depending on your viewpoint, glaring example of this knack is his treatment of the ever-resilient Macbeth. Confronted by the chroniclers' quarrel between the generous, traditional Celtic king and a murderous regicide and tyrant, Boece elaborated. To him we owe the witches who prophecy Macbeth's fate and the ghost of Banquo, who provided a fictional genealogy for the later Stewart kings. This and much else besides was absorbed wholesale from Boece into Holinshed's *Chronicles of England, Scotland and Ireland* later in the century.

Yet Hector Boece's overall treatment of Macbeth cannot be historically dismissed. The historian was guided by Scotland's aversion to tyranny, as embodied in that prime historical record, the 1321 Declaration of Arbroath. Boece's Macbeth has a legitimate claim to the throne as a 'tanist', ie one who is close through family to the monarch and can be appointed to rule. In other words,

Boece judges Macbeth by the standards of his time rather than according to the emphasis on primogeniture which the Canmore dynasty applied in Scotland from Margaret onwards.

Boece had a big influence on his successor historians and writers, especially the formidable George Buchanan who shone as both historian and poet. In the European mainstream, Hector continued to be admired despite sniping from rival English historians. He is buried in the magnificent King's College Chapel in Aberdeen, given pride of place beside his illustrious patron, Bishop Elphinstone.

David Lindsay

If Hector Boece gives us a broad-brush portrait of Scotland, poet and dramatist Sir David Lindsay provides much fuller and grittier close-ups. Lindsay was a Fife landowner connected with the Earls of Crawford. He went into court service as a youngster and remained there most of his working life, first as a gentleman usher, and then as a Lyon Herald and diplomat. He is in some ways the ultimate insider, personally close to James v, yet he has his finger on the social pulse and addresses the state of the nation, which he calls 'the community of the realm'. Like Boece, Lindsay is a reformer, but one influenced by Protestant ideas.

Lindsay's early poems use inherited poetic forms – dream visions, allegories and complaints – with sober plain-speaking about abuses of royal power, the law and especially the Church. He is not theologically minded but focussed on morals and their social impact. His religious references are Lutheran in tone, based on the example of Christ. But the social commentary is direct and detailed, making Lindsay an explicitly political writer.

Lindsay's originality becomes clearer with his 'The Testament and Complaint of Our Soverane Lordis Papyngo'. Using humour, dialogue and pawky characterisation, the poet puts across his bread-and-butter issues with a leaven of dramatic wit. The king's parrot delivers lots of advice to the young James v, including the books of poetry, history and good counsel which he ought to be reading in preparation for his role. But then the papyngo manages to fall off a tree and lies mortally injured. Three clerics come to his aid in the shape of a magpie, a raven and a kite, supposedly to bring pious comfort and administer the last rites. Instead they tear the poor papyngo to pieces, seizing even his heart, which he has just bequeathed to the king. The beast fable is less subtle than Henryson, but gets Lindsay's point across.

It was probably at Epiphany in 1540 that Lindsay's first drama was performed at the court in Linlithgow Palace. This seems to have been an early version of his later extended Morality play *Ane Satire of the Thrie Estaitis* – the Nobility, the Church and the Burghs. No text survives, but we have a description recorded by a spectator who sent their account to the English ambassador.

It is clear that the Epiphany interlude was an outright demand for reform, articulated by Lindsay through the poor, who are being oppressed by those who are supposed to help them: the Church. James v was present at the performance and threatens the leading churchmen, who were also in attendance, with the treatment being dished out by his uncle Henry viii to the English Church.

Yet James himself does not come off unscathed, as the government is colluding with the Church and profiting from its wealth. The Poor Man, a leading character in the interlude, denies that the king in the play is legitimate, because only God is the true ruler.

Then, looking directly at the real James, the player says that the true king has hanged Johnny Armstrong and his famous Border outlaws. This neatly manages to compliment James v on upholding law and order, in this case anyway, while reminding him that he is subject to God. It is bold theatre and politics.

James' commitment to reform, however, remained half-hearted. Like most of the Stewart kings, he had an attachment to traditional Catholic devotions. Also, he had no motivation to dismantle church structures and seize assets since, unlike Henry VIII, he and his relations already controlled the major abbacies and bishoprics through their inappropriate appointment to church offices. When a Protestant Reformation eventually succeeded in Scotland, the aristocracy simply took ownership of the property and lands which they already controlled.

Lindsay was frustrated by the King's lack of action and became an increasingly committed Protestant. He was closely involved in the dramatic events which unfolded after James v's untimely death in 1542. This was effectively a first attempt at a Reformation, and we shall pick up that thread with the historians shortly. Subsequently, after leaving Court office, Lindsay staged two large-scale, public performances of his now much expanded Morality drama, one in Cupar in 1552 and one in Edinburgh in 1554.

Ane Satire of the Thrie Estaitis starts like a conventional Morality concerned with the education of a young ruler, and the battle for influence between the Virtues and the Vices, as the Parliament or Three Estates of the realm are about to meet. The traditional form is delivered by Lindsay with vigour and gusto, deploying a skilful range of spoken Scots. Chastitie finds herself exiled and homeless, and addresses the Bishops or Lords Spiritual.

CHASTITIE

My Lords, laud, gloir, triumph and reverence
Mot be unto your halie Spirituall stait!
I yow beseik of your benevolence
To harbry me that am sa desolait.
Lords, I have past throw mony uncouth schire,
But in this land I can get na ludgeing.
Of my name gif ye wald haif knawledging,
Forsuith, my Lords, they call me Chastitie.
I you beseik, of your graces bening (kindness).
Give me ludgeing this nicht, for charitie.

SPIRITUALITIE

Pass on, Madame, we knaw you nocht;
Or be Him that the warld hes wrocht,
Your cumming shall be richt deir coft (bought)
Gif ye mak langer tarrie.

ABBOT

But (without) doubt we will baith leif and die
With our luif Sensualitie:
We will haif nae mair deal with thee
Than with the Queene of Faerie.

A Tailor and his friend, or 'gossop', the shoemaker, reflect on chastity in a more forthright idiom.

TAYLOUR

Alace, gossop, alace, how stands with you?
Yon cankart carlin (witch), alace, hes brokin my
    brow.

Now weils (prosper) you, prietis, now weils you all
  your lifes,
That ar nocht weddit with sic wicket wyfes!
SOWTAR
Bischops ar blist, howbeit that thae be waryit (cursed),
For thay may fuck their fill and be unmaryit!

An interlude between the acts is a play within the play. A pauper whose elderly parents have died laments that the priest has taken both of his cows to pay for the funerals. A Pardoner then pretends to offer his assistance, while seeking to defraud the pauper of his last penny.

The second act of *Ane Satire* moves from Morality into uncharted theatrical terrain. The Three Estates assemble with the Lords Spiritual processing backwards into the action. As things get underway, John Commonweal, the play's Everyman, leaps the barricades to challenge the gathered lords, burghers and bishops on behalf of the common people.

REX
Schwa me thy name, gudeman, I thee command.
JOHN
Marie, John the Common-weil of fair Scotland.
REX
The Common-weil has bene amang his fais (foes)!
JOHN
Ye, sir, that gars the Common-weil want clais (clothes).
REX
What is the caus the Common-weil is crukit?

JOHN
Because the Common-weil hes bene overlukit.
REX
What gars thee luik sa with ane dreirie hert?
JOHN
Because the Thrie Estaitis gangs all backwart.

The Parliament proceeds to debate and approve detailed reforms, until the whole occasion is upended by the riotous entry of the Fool. He then delivers his own Sermon on Folly, which undermines everything that has gone before, while pleasing the crowd – which proves his case that Folly rules supreme, not the king or God!

Ane Satire of the Thrie Estaitis may include features that the playwright had observed on his diplomatic travels. It is one of Europe's great late-medieval dramas, and a significant mouthpiece for social reform. Lindsay's play is also a defining Scottish drama to the present day. Everything Sir David knew about Scottish life and international politics goes into the mix, and the scale of his achievement remains astonishing. He does for theatre what he and others had done for poetry, modifying traditional forms through Scots realism and humour.

Yet *Ane Satire* also owes its importance to timing. The play could not have emerged in this form without Lindsay's driving convictions about national reform. To understand this we have to place his work within the wider drama of Scotland's Reformation struggle. And to that we must turn to a Scottish writer whose literary achievement is little understood.

John Knox the Author

John Knox was the leading advocate, spokesperson, propagandist and, in due course, recorder of the Scottish Reformation. His religious views were and are divisive. Knox was not a theologian of the first rank, but he was a very effective communicator in speech and print. It is as a vivid writer and champion of key ideas that John Knox deserves a place in Scotland's literary pantheon.

Knox's writings include letters (public and private), sermons, tracts and history. His letters could deliver pastoral comfort, often to women friends, as well as public admonition, often to queens. He is a forceful controversialist, as in his notorious *The First Blast of the Trumpet Against the Monstrous Regiment (Unnatural Rule) of Women*, and his less well-known but equally full-on diatribe against Baptists. But Knox's most impressive and enduring work is his *Historie of the Reformation of Religion in Scotland*. Knox himself realised this book was his principal legacy and he was still dictating later chapters when he died in 1572 in Edinburgh, probably in the house which still bears his name.

'History' in this case is a relative term, since Knox's book is as much memoir or apologia as history, expressing a fiery defence of his actions and ideas. For the prophet of Protestant reform, this was personal and he was determined to put his testimony down in writing. Paradoxically, it is that personal drive which makes Knox's work powerful early modern literature. Parts can be read like a novel as well as history.

John Knox was born in Haddington to parents of what he called the 'midling' sort. As a youngster he went from Haddington Grammar School to the University of St Andrews, where he was taught by John Major the philosopher, who also came from humble East Lothian origins. Knox proved a very capable student, and he was ordained as a priest below the statutory age by special dispensation of the Pope. Then he ran aground. Lacking aristocratic connections or patronage, Knox was unable to secure a paid position in the late medieval Church. Instead, he returned to East Lothian, and worked as a tutor and as a notary or lawyer's assistant.

At St Andrews, Knox had access to Protestant ideas through students who had been abroad, and through the close trading relationships across the Baltic and North Seas. Some of the East Lothian lairds or gentry were sympathetic to Lutheran ideas, including translation of the Bible into vernacular languages and reform of the Church. Particularly contentious was the sale of 'pardons' which would shorten your time in purgatory, like an advance deposit on heaven. There was also widespread criticism of wealth and luxury in the monasteries, while religious vocations declined steeply. But burgh churches were generally flourishing and most towns also supported friaries. Some argued that the Church could and should reform itself without adopting radical Protestant beliefs.

Knox began to write his account of Protestantism in Scotland as he returned from exile in Geneva, and the Calvinist Reformation took shape in 1559–60. He writes with an awareness of Boece and Bellenden, but from the off Knox is in conviction mode.

This tyranny notwithstanding, the knowledge of God did wondrously increase within this realm, partly by reading, partly by brotherly conference, which in those dangerous days was used to the comfort of many; but chiefly by merchants and mariners, who, frequenting other countries, heard the true doctrine affirmed, and the vanity of the papistical religion openly rebuked. Dundee and Leith were the principal centres of enlightenment, and there David Beaton, cruel Cardinal, made a very strait inquisition, divers being compelled to abjure and burn their bills, some in St Andrews, and some at Edinburgh [...] This was done for a spectacle and triumph to Mary of Lorraine, lately arrived from France, as wife of James the Fifth, King of Scots. What plagues she brought with her, and how they yet continue, may be manifestly seen by such as are not blind.

The rage of these bloody beasts proceeded so that the King's Court itself escaped not danger; for in it divers were suspected, and some were accused. And yet ever did some light burst out in the midst of darkness; for the truth of Christ Jesus entered even into the cloisters, as well of Friars, as of Monks and Canons. John Linn, a Grey Friar, left his hypocritical habit and the den of those murderers the Grey Friars. A Black Friar, called Friar Kyllour, set forth the history of Christ's Passion in the form of a play, which he both preached and practised openly in Stirling, the King himself being present, upon a Good Friday in the morning.

Books and plays were both deployed in these first conflicts. The Reformation was to become a battle of words, and Knox aimed to get his version of events down first. In consequence, he remains a main primary source, though one whose bias is unconcealed.

Having covered the death of James v following the collapse of his campaign against England at Solway Moss, Knox follows the twists and turns as the Earl of Arran becomes Regent. Cardinal Beaton and James' widow, Marie de Guise, support a Catholic alliance with France, but the Earl of Douglas champions a Protestant alliance with England. This sounds rather like Scottish business as normal until the entry of George Wishart, 'that blessed martyr of God', into the narrative in 1544. Suddenly, Knox is writing about events which he experienced.

After preaching in Angus and Dundee, where he comforted plague victims and survived an assassination attempt, the Lutheran reformer Wishart came to Edinburgh and then East Lothian. He was welcomed to the Douglas household in Longniddry, where Knox was the tutor. He preached at Tranent and went on to Haddington where the Earl of Bothwell, an ally and suitor of Marie de Guise, banned people from attending. But Wishart went ahead and Knox found him pacing behind the high altar before preaching to a small congregation.

'O Lord, how long shall it be that Thy holy Word shall be despised, and men shall not regard their own salvation. I have heard of thee, Haddington, that in thee two or three thousand people would have been at a vain clerk play; and now, to hear the messenger of the Eternal God, of all thy town or parish there cannot be numbered a hundred persons.'

Knox was now acting as a personal bodyguard for Wishart, carrying a two-handed sword. All the danger signs were flashing, and Wishart delivered an ominous prophecy to the Haddington faithful, which sadly came to pass in the same decade.

Sore and fearful shall the plague be that shall ensue this thy
contempt: with fire and sword thou shalt be plagued; yea,
thou Haddington, in special, strangers shall possess thee,
and you, the present inhabitants, shall either in bondage
serve your enemies, or else ye shall be chased from your own
habitations; and that because ye have not known, and will
not know, the time of God's merciful visitation.

Then, that same night, Bothwell struck in events that were to
change Knox's own life.

The manner of Master George Wishart's taking was thus:
departing from Haddington, he took his good-night, as it
were for ever, of all his acquaintance, especially from Hugh
Douglas of Longniddry. John Knox pressing to go with him,
Master George said, 'Nay return to your bairns and God
bless you. *Ane is eneuch* for a sacrifice.' He then caused a
two-handed sword, which commonly was with him, to be
taken from John Knox, who, albeit unwillingly, obeyed and
returned with Hugh Douglas. Master George passed on foot
– for it was a vehement frost – to Ormiston. After supper, he
merrily said, 'Methinks that I desire earnestly to sleep'; and
'Will we sing a Psalm?' So he appointed the fifty-first Psalm,
which began thus in Scottish metre, 'Have mercy on me now,
good Lord' [...] Which being ended he passed to his chamber
with these words, 'God grant quiet rest'. Before midnight the
place was beset about so that none could escape.

This is as dramatic as David Lindsay, yet driven by Knox's own psychological investment. There are also more Scots idioms, as in my italicised 'ane is eneuch', at work in these passages than the printed texts reflect.

The trial and savage execution of Wishart in St Andrews comes next, followed by the brutal assassination of Cardinal Beaton, whose body is slung over the castle wall and pissed upon, with no lack of colloquial vigour. Knox is clearly drawing on eyewitness accounts here, including that of William Kirkcaldy of Grange, who was to become his friend and ally.

Soon the Protestant occupation of St Andrews Castle drew Knox and David Lindsay into the same orbit. Knox joined the garrison where he experienced a 'calling' to become a preacher, stepping into the place left vacant by his role model, Wishart. Did Knox feel guilt at abandoning him in his hour of need? Meanwhile, Lindsay had been appointed by Regent Arran to negotiate with the garrison, many of whom were Fife lairds well known to the Lyon Herald.

Negotiations failed, and St Andrews Castle was bombarded into submission by a French fleet. Knox was captured and spent 18 months rowing in the galleys. Then he went into a long exile in England and on the continent until the Calvinist Reformation in Scotland in 1559 brought him home from Geneva to become Minister of St Giles Church in Edinburgh.

All of this can be found in *The Historie* along with a continuity narrative about Scotland which uses diverse styles, including vivid drama and evocative descriptions, even when Knox is not personally involved. Consider the knockabout glee of this account of a Protestant riot in Edinburgh on St Giles Day 1558. This blends physical comedy with sarcastic disdain.

Yet the priests and Friars would not cease to have that great
solemnity and manifest abomination which they customly
had upon Saint Giles's day. They would have that idol borne;
and therefore all necessary preparation was duly made. A
marmoset idol [...] was fast fixed with iron nails upon a
barrow, called their fertour. There assembled priests, Friars,
Canons, and rotten Papists, with tabors and trumpets,
banners and bagpipes, and who was there to lead the ring,
but the Queen Regent herself, with all her shavelings, for
honour of that feast. West about it went, and came down
the High Street, and down to the Canon Cross. The Queen
Regent dined that day in Sandy Carpetyne's house, betwixt
the Bows, and immediately after the Queen had entered the
lodging, some of those that were in the enterprise drew nigh
to the idol, as if willing to help to bear him, and getting the
fertour upon their shoulders, began to shudder, thinking that
thereby the idol should have fallen. But that was provided
for and prevented by the iron nails, as we have said; and so
one began to cry, 'Down with the idol; down with it!' and
without delay it was pulled down. One took him by the
heels and, dadding his head on the causeway, left Dagon
without head or hands, and cried, 'Fie upon thee, thou
young Saint Giles, thy father would have tarried four such.'
[...] Down went the crosses, off went the surplice, and the
round caps cornered with the crowns. The Grey Friars
gaped, the Black Friars blew, the priests panted and fled, and
happy was he that first reached the house; such a sudden
fray amongst the generation of Antichrist within this realm
never came before.

Marie de Guise was overthrown the following year and died in Edinburgh Castle, where her body lay neglected in the then ruinous St Margaret's Chapel.

Also absorbed into *The Historie* are the founding documents of the Calvinist Reformation, which John Knox co-authored. *The Scots Confession*, which was approved by the Three Estates, and the radical social blueprint *The First Book of Discipline*, which the nobility vetoed, are masterpieces of compressed eloquence which were to influence ideas far beyond Scotland.

The rejection of a radical Calvinist order by the Protestant nobility emßbittered Knox, who came to feel that the ensuing power struggle between James Stewart Earl of Moray and Mary Queen of Scots was a betrayal on both fronts. Knox resumed writing *The Historie* later in the 1560s when his agenda was in ashes: the wealth of the old Church had not been applied to education or care of the poor, and there was an active threat of Roman Catholic counter-reformation, not least through the potential influence of Mary. She had returned in 1561 after the unexpected death of her young husband, King Francis, to assume power in Scotland – the Catholic monarch of a now officially Protestant nation, already governed by her illegitimate half-brother James Stewart, later the Earl of Moray.

In consequence, the later parts of Knox's History are more angry than triumphal. Yet they are also enriched by pages of dramatic dialogue, embodying Knox's version of his disputes with Mary Queen of Scots, her Secretary Maitland of Lethington and other leading players in this theatre of power. One flash point is the question of who Mary will marry.

KNOX: God hath not sent me to wait upon the courts of
princesses, or upon the chambers of ladies. I am sent to
preach the Evangel of Jesus Christ to such as please to hear
it. [...] But the most part of your Nobility are so addicted
to your affections, that neither God, His Word, nor yet their
commonwealth are rightly regarded. Therefore it becomes me
so to speak, that they may know their duty.

QUEEN: What have ye to do with my marriage? Or what are
ye within this commonwealth?

KNOX: A subject born within the same, Madam. And, albeit I
be neither Earl, Lord, nor Baron within it, God has made me
a profitable member within the same, however abject I be in
your eyes.

Despite his advocacy of individual conscience, Knox espoused
patriarchy and in a patriarchal age it was presumed that Mary's
husband would become king. Her eventual choice of her cousin,
Henry Stewart, Lord Darnley, pleased no-one. He was a nominal
Catholic, a Stewart in the royal succession of England and Scotland,
and unapproved by Elizabeth I. To cap all, Mary acknowledged
him as her consort, but not as a joint ruler, far less her superior.

Serious troubles lay ahead, but to understand the plot, we
have to switch narrators to another major Scottish writer, leaving
Knox in permanent dispute mode.

George Buchanan

One of the few who were pleased by Mary's marriage was her court poet, George Buchanan. He owed a traditional loyalty to Darnley's family, the Lennox Stewarts, who ruled as earls in the area in which he had been brought up, south of Loch Lomond. Though a younger son of a modest family, Buchanan had studied under John Major in St Andrews and Paris, and become a brilliant academic. His own students included Montaigne, the French humanist, and for a time he was tutor to one of James V's illegitimate sons.

George Buchanan was also a consummate linguist, and his reputation as a poet, translator, historian and dramatist was to outgrow his eminent status as a teacher. Buchanan's standing was Europe-wide, but he holds a unique place in Scottish literature as the pre-eminent 16th-century historian, a first rank poet, a political thinker and a leading reformer. Yet because Buchanan wrote in Latin, the *lingua franca* of his time, he is less read today than even John Knox.

Though a convert to the Protestant cause, Buchanan remains a classical humanist in the European tradition. His arguments are based on legal, moral and political principles, unlike Knox who always appealed to a Calvinist reading of the Bible as his ultimate authority. Having taught in France and Portugal, Buchanan became a court poet during Mary's reign as Queen of France, and he returned with her to Scotland. There he continued in his role as part of Mary's court, while also involving himself in reform of Scotland's universities, which he regarded as still bound to old-fashioned scholastic ways rather than the new, progressive humanism. In these efforts he was supported by the influential Earl of Moray.

In France, George Buchanan had been enthusiastic in praising Mary as a girl who shone as 'both nature's work and art's.' His 'Epithalium' for Mary's marriage to the Dauphin Francois lauds both royal houses and nations, and elevates the union as worthy of not just historical but mythological praises. Back in Scotland, with Mary now a young Queen in her own right, Buchanan presented her with the first edition of his translation of the Hebrew Psalms into Latin, which was to become one of his most celebrated works. This was accompanied by a dedicatory poem, which reads in literal translation as follows.

> O dear lady, you now hold the sceptre of Scotland,
> Bequeathed to you by countless royal ancestors.
> You surpass your allotted place in life by your
> merits, your years and virtues.
> Your sex by your powers of mind, and your nobility
> of birth by your character.
> Receive with good grace the psalms re-formed in Latin
> verse,
> The fine artistry of the prophetic king.
> My labours undertaken far from Cirrha, and the
> Muses' sacred Permessian waters,
> Born as if under the star of the northern sky,
> I did not dare expose like an ill-begotten child,
> Lest I should seem to be displeased by what pleased you.
> For what they could not hope for from their author's
> skill,
> They may perhaps owe to your kindly spirit.

Mary's marriage to Henry Stewart, Lord Darnley, became the subject of another court poem, addressed to Henry 'the best of kings'. If things go well for him, opines Buchanan, then his kingdom will prosper too. These words read ominously in retrospect. In fact, even the kingly dedication jars since Mary refused to allow Darnley to call himself king. She quickly came to realise that he was jealous and scheming to supplant her authority. Tragic cracks were already appearing in the shining façade of this royal dream alliance.

The birth of Mary's longed-for son and heir, Prince James, in 1566 might reasonably have mended matters; instead it made things worse. Darnley was psychotically jealous of the baby, even in his mother's womb. This may not have been entirely paranoia, however, since after James' safe arrival, Mary moved to limit the damage Darnley was causing to her government.

Crucially, Darnley had become the weak link in Mary's defences, exposing her to the machinations of her half-brother, Moray, who was often acting in concert with William Cecil, Elizabeth I's Secretary of State, all behind Elizabeth's back. Also in play was the powerful Douglas faction led by the Earl of Morton. Darnley was both a Tudor and a Douglas through his mother, and a Stewart through his father, Lennox.

Working together, Mary's opponents used Darnley's resentment and gullibility to engineer the assassination of her Secretary, David Rizzio. This bloody act in Mary's private apartments was a warning to the young Queen, and perhaps aimed at making her miscarry. Through a terrifying night trapped at Holyrood, she managed to convince Darnley that the conspirators had no intention of making Darnley king, but of discarding him when his usefulness was over. Then she escaped and rode, heavily pregnant, to Dunbar, where she was given refuge and support by the Earl of Bothwell – son of the Earl who had wooed Mary's mother and arrested George Wishart.

Many of those implicated in the Rizzio murder went into exile and planned their revenge. Yet again, they worked on Darnley, promising to overthrow Mary and put him on the throne, as long as he did the bidding of Moray and Morton. Maitland of Lethington was involved this time too, with the aim of freeing Mary from Darnley, as was Bothwell, who was aiming to supplant Darnley as Mary's husband. Mary and her child were sitting in a nest of vipers.

Darnley was completely taken in, and his sanity was by now in question. Having been treated for syphilis in Glasgow, he was brought back to Edinburgh, insisting on going to Kirk O' Field House where the cellars had been packed with gunpowder. Mary was to stay that night and be blown up, while Darnley escaped. However, on the night in question, Mary delayed at a wedding party for two of her servants and chose to stay on at Holyrood.

The quick-thinking Bothwell set out for nearby Kirk O' Field with a torchlit escort to give the impression that Mary was coming, albeit late. Darnley then instructed his servant to light a long fuse and he was lowered out of the window in a chair, dressed in his night clothes, into an orchard just outside the town wall. There, his Douglas relations were waiting, as he thought, to carry him off to safety and kingship. Instead, they strangled him and left his body beneath a tree. Then the house went up with an enormous explosion that shook the whole of Edinburgh and was heard at Holyrood.

Stage two of the core plot, now a double- or triple-cross, was to blame Bothwell for the murder and accuse him of being in cahoots with Mary, whom the pre-prepared propaganda implied was in an adulterous relationship with the Earl. She had, in effect, warmed him up to step into the royal vacancy. The murder of Darnley was, as intended, disastrous for Mary's reputation at home and internationally. It also potentially called James' legitimacy into question. Mary fell into the trap as devised. Friendless and surrounded by violent threats, she leaned on the ever-loyal, macho Bothwell, who then pressed her into marriage. Only later did he confess to his appalled wife the prominent part he had played in Darnley's assassination.

But there were unexpected twists. After the new marriage, Bothwell was put to flight and Mary herself was arrested. Imprisoned in Lochleven Castle, where she miscarried Bothwell's twins, she was forced to abdicate. She then escaped, raised an army that was defeated at Langside and fled to England to throw herself on cousin Elizabeth's mercy. Elizabeth was ultra-cautious, and unaware that William Cecil had been involved with Moray in the overthrow of a divinely appointed Queen. She demanded to know what proof there was of Mary's involvement in Darnley's murder.

No Scottish story has attracted more attention than the drama of Mary Queen of Scots. But from the beginning it is a literary creation. Initially, it is a triumph of black yet crude propaganda – sex and murder at the palace. On a tabloid level, this was irresistible. John Knox was not in on the plot, as the conspirators regarded him as politically naïve, but he swallowed the propaganda hook, line and sinker, becoming a virulent advocate of Mary's execution for adultery and regicide.

George Buchanan was not in on the advance plot either due to his Darnley loyalties, but he quickly became the principal architect of a detailed case against Mary. Along with Moray's Secretary, James Wood, Buchanan devised a paper trail to prove Mary's guilt. This involved doctoring her correspondence and re-dating the sequence to demonstrate that Mary had foreknowledge of 'Bothwell's plan' to kill Darnley. Even Cecil, who hated and feared Mary, realised it would not bear close examination and Mary was never brought to trial on these charges. Instead, she was left in prison without trial for 18 years.

Yet Buchanan's devastating, detailed public account in his *Detection of Mary Queen of Scots*, largely repeated in his later *History*, so blackened Mary's name that to the present day the popular view is that she was in some way involved in Darnley's murder and/or in an improper relationship with Bothwell. Yet Buchanan's denunciation is well over-the-top, asserting even that Darnley's illness in Glasgow was the consequence of Mary trying to poison him. The treatment with mercury had of course been previously kept from public view. There is no hard evidence of Mary's involvement, only implication and innuendo.

Did George Buchanan believe his own literary plotline? Possibly. Did he understand its impact on Mary? Certainly, for he was resolved to revenge Darnley's death, and to treat the infant James as his father' son, labelling his mother as 'a whore'. This was for political and religious reasons, but somewhere too there was a personal canker. Had Buchanan, and perhaps Knox, been on some level charmed by the young Queen's beauty and ability, making the kickback sexually charged and repressed?

So successful were Buchanan's efforts that when Shakespeare

became interested in James VI of Scotland as Elizabeth's likely successor and a potential patron, he chose Holinshed's version of Macbeth and the Danish legend of Hamlet as promising subjects. While Macbeth, as rewritten by Hector Boece, played to James' obsessions with witchcraft and the murder of kings, Hamlet is even closer to the young king's own life, as written and directly taught to James by George Buchanan.

The Prince of Denmark's father has been murdered by his mother's adulterous lover, whom she then marries and makes king. Theatre appears to mimic life, or at least Buchanan's version of events. To cap the connections, James VI married Anne of Denmark and they spent their honeymoon at Hamlet's castle in Elsinore. When Shakespeare's theatre company toured to Edinburgh, James VI had a temporary theatre constructed for them in Blackfriars Street, in defiance of the Town Council's ban on theatre. Did he race up when they arrived to give them, like Hamlet, his views on acting, in the same way as James had instructed his poets how to write?

John Knox was still trying to come to terms with the Darnley murder on his deathbed. By this time, his old friend William Kirkcaldy of Grange had switched sides, realising that the charges against Mary were a tissue of lies. He was holding Edinburgh Castle for Queen Mary, though she was imprisoned in England. Moray had been assassinated. The Earl of Morton, head of the House of Douglas, was about to become Regent and came to pay his respects to the ailing reformer. 'Did you have any part in Darnley's murder?' demanded Knox. 'No', replied Morton, who ordered the actual deed. Morton stumbled down the outside stair visibly shaken, yet he gave the eulogy at Knox's funeral in St Giles

Church. When James VI came of age, he had Morton guillotined for his part in the murder.

Before his death, Knox denounced the Queen's Men in the castle by personal letter, prophesying that Kirkcaldy would 'swing in the face of the sun'. Eventually, Edinburgh Castle was blasted into submission by English artillery and Kirkcaldy was sentenced to death, despite a huge effort by friends and foes to ransom the life of Scotland's 'most gallant gentleman'. He knew too much to live.

John Knox left his *Historie* unfinished, but he achieved his aim of shaping the Reformation narrative for future generations. In this he was aided by George Buchanan, whose magisterial *History of Scotland* was published in Edinburgh shortly before his own death in 1582. Buchanan's nephew Thomas, along with his university friend Andrew Melville, came to visit the old man in his house off the High Street by The Tron.

Buchanan sent them down to the Canongate to find out how the *History* was progressing at the printers. The two students returned with the news that Arbuthnott, the printer, had stopped the press at the section on Darnley's murder, fearing that James would be angered by Buchanan's account of his mother. 'Have I told the truth?' demanded the old controversialist. 'Yes, I think so, sir,' replied Thomas, whose options in this dialogue may have been limited. 'Then I will abide the King's feud, and that of all his kin.' In other words, 'print and be damned', though the choice of words, given Buchanan's original family loyalty to the Lennox Stewarts, is interesting.

James VI did not approve, and the *History* was burnt at Edinburgh's Mercat Cross. Ideas, however, cannot be burnt.

Buchanan's views on constitutional monarchy had wide influence, especially his insistence that ruler and ruled alike are subject to the law. They helped shape the American constitution and contemporary Scottish politics. These ideas are encapsulated in Buchanan's political treatise *De Jure Regni apud Scotos* – on the law or rule or kingship – but they are expounded through the narrative of the *History*.

Buchanan was also the first historian to deal seriously with the Picts and to understand the diverse linguistic side of Scottish culture – coming from the Lennox he was a native Gaelic speaker. His cultural legacy was lasting, not least his emphasis on poetry being spoken aloud in its original language, his insistence on the value of drama in education despite Presbyterian suspicions and his high valuation of the classics as contemporary models. Buchanan's own Latin plays became the foundation of French neo-classical theatre. James VI was to be shaped by all these values through Buchanan's tutoring.

Finally, it is worth noting that, on Scottish independence, George Buchanan emphatically sided with Hector Boece against John Major. He also coined the phrase 'perfervidum ingenium Scotorum' – the fervent spirit/genius of the Scots. Undoubtedly Buchanan, with all his international learning, was as proud and prickly a Scot as any in his time or since. He is buried in Greyfriars Kirkyard in Edinburgh.

SIX

The 17th Century: Other Worlds

Hawthornden

THE TRANSLATION OF James VI from Edinburgh to London in 1603, to become King of Britain and Ireland, removed Scotland's main focus of literary patronage, its royal court. James took his love of literature and language with him, becoming the patron of Shakespeare's company and initiating the King James Bible, later known as the Authorized Version. His theatre-loving consort, Anne, also supported drama and court masque.

George Buchanan's unrelenting routine in James' schoolroom at Stirling Castle had comprised Greek before porridge, with Cicero, Livy and history before lunch, to be followed by composition, arithmetic, cosmography, logic and rhetoric, and potentially some Hebrew for light relief. This produced the most intellectual monarch yet to reign in these islands. But Buchanan's denigration of James' mother, Mary Queen of Scots, did lasting psychological damage. And his insistence on the doctrine of limited monarchy had the opposite effect from that intended; James became an ardent advocate of royal rule 'by divine right', penning a treatise on the matter for his children. Again the long term impacts were severe, as Charles I followed his grandmother to the chopping block and his son James VII and II was overthrown.

The core problem was that the official triumph of Protestantism under James VI and I produced as many questions as answers, especially in his northern kingdom. How was the new Church to be governed? What were to be the roles of monarch and parliaments?

And who was in charge of royal succession in a united monarchy?

Despite James' best efforts to realise a full union between England and Scotland, the English parliament refused to accept Scots as citizens with equal rights. Consequently, until the 1707 Union of Parliaments, Scotland was ruled by monarchs in London without political representation or equal trading privileges. This led to endless complications when the Wars of the Three Kingdoms, popularly and inaccurately labelled the English Civil War, broke out in 1639. In one shape or form, these bloody struggles continued in Scotland until 1689, when there was another supposedly long-term settlement of politics and religion. As a result of these conflicts, literature was pushed into the background in the 1600s. It had less national importance than in any previous century or those to come; the question was one of survival, whether as an elite or counter-cultural activity, or both.

The longest surviving member of James VI's Castalian Band of poets in Scotland was William Drummond. He was the nephew of another Castalian, William Fowler, who became Queen Anne's Secretary and moved to London. In 1610 Drummond inherited his father's estate of Hawthornden in Roslin Glen on the North Esk, just south of Edinburgh. He then retired to the leafy shades and devoted his life to poetry, reading, meditation and music.

> Thrice happie he, who by some shadie Grove,
> Fare from the clamorous World, doth live his owne,
> Though solitarie, who is not alone,
> But doth converse with that Eternall Love [...]
> The World is full of Horrours, Troubles, Slights,
> Woods harmelesse Shades have only true Delightes.

Drummond was a skilful sonneteer, but also a fine madrigalist, probably singing to his own accompaniment on the lute. These are hymns to beauty underlaid by an awareness of fragility and the marks of time.

> Now doth the Sunne appear,
> The Mountaines Snowes decay,
> Crown'd with fraile Flowres forth comes the Babye
>   yeare.
> My Soule, Time postes away,
> And thou yet in that Frost
> Which Flowre and fruit hath lost,
> As if all here immortall were, dost stay:
> For shame thy Powers awake,
> Looke to that Heaven which never Night makes blacke,
> And there, at that immortall Sunnes bright Rayes,
> Decke thee with Flowers which feare not rage of Dayes.

Both Drummond's verse and his prose reflections are tinged with melancholy and religious resignation. Yet he also continued as a kind of unofficial Scottish laureate, producing a major elegy on the death of James VI and I's eldest son, Prince Henry, and a celebration of James' one and only return visit to his native Edinburgh in 1617.

The uneasy relationship between James' two royal capitals and kingdoms is encapsulated in Ben Jonson's visit to Scotland, when he stayed at Hawthornden over Christmas and New Year 1618–9. Jonson was the leading neo-classical poet and playwright in English Literature, a deviser of masques for Queen Anne and the dominant pundit in literary London. He was also physically massive, loud, intemperate and a giant consumer of food and drink. Jonson had walked the 400 miles from London, taking in a visit to the western Borders where his father had originated. Ben's impact on the peaceful shades of Hawthornden can be imagined!

The meticulous Drummond dutifully recorded the great man's unguarded table talk, while Jonson pontificated as if holding court in one of London's literary watering holes.

The King (James I) said Sir Philip Sydney was no poet...
He (Jonson) said to the King that his master Mr George Buchanan, had corrupted his ear when young, and learnt him to sing verses when he should have read them.

Queen Elizabeth never saw herself after she became old in a true glass; they painted her and would sometimes vermilion her nose.

The Earl of Leicester gave a bottle of liquor to his lady, which he willed her to use in any faintness; which she after his return from Court, not knowing it was poison, gave him, and so he died.

That in the papers Sir Walter Raleigh had (from Spenser) of the Allegories of his Faerie Queene, by the 'Blatant Beast' the Puritans were understood, by the 'False Duessa' the Queen of Scots.

That Shakespeare wanted art [...] in a play he brought in a number of men saying they had suffered shipwreck in Bohemia, where there is no sea, not by a hundred miles.

My Lord Chancellor of England (Francis Bacon) wringeth his speeches from the strings of his band, and other counsellors from the picking of their teeth.

That Donne's (John Donne) Anniversary was profane and

full of blasphemies [...] he told Mr Donne that if he had
written of the Virgin Mary, it had been something.

And so forth. Jonson also read from his own and others' work,
and informed Drummond that, though his verses were good, 'they
smelled too much of the Schools, and were not after the fancy of
the time.' For his part, Drummond followed up the visit with
complimentary letters, but confided in his private Memoranda
with a rather different assessment.

> He is a great lover and praiser of himself; a contemner
> and scorner of others; given rather to lose a friend than a
> jest; jealous of every word and action of those about him
> (especially after drink, which is one of the elements in which
> he liveth); a dissembler of ill parts which reign in him, a
> bragger of some good he wanteth; thinketh nothing well but
> what either he himself or one of his countrymen hath said or
> done [...] For any religion, being versed in both (Protestant
> and Catholic). Interpreteth best sayings and deeds often to the
> worst. Oppressd with phantasy, which hath ever mastered his
> reason, a general disease in many poets. His inventions are
> smooth and easy; but above all he excelleth in Translation.

These private journals contain Drummond's best prose, but were
unpublishable. It does seem that Ben may have outstayed his
welcome by the Esk.

Flights of Language

While James continued to rule his subordinate kingdom, as he boasted, 'by the stroke of his pen', writers were finding unofficial outlets. In addition to private journals, travel offered another form of escape from Scotland's uneasy state. William Lithgow combined poetry with travel writing in a vigorous and distinctive style. Like Drummond, he wrote a poem about James' welcome to Edinburgh in 1617 and then, before departing for foreign climes, he made his feelings about Scotland clear.

> To thee, o dearest soyle, these mourning lines I bring,
> And with a broken bleeding breast, my sad farewell I sing
> [...]
> Since on the planets of my plaints, I move about the Pole.
> ....
> And, Scotland, I attest, my witnesse reigns above,
> In all my worlde-wide wandring ways, I kept to thee my love;
> To many forraine breastes, in these exiling dayes,
> In sympathizing harmonies, I sung thine endless prayse;
> And where thou wast not knowne, I registred thy name,
> Within their annalles of renowne to eternize thy fame.

This wandering Scot remains a staunch patriot, but Lithgow was not the pining sort and his *Rare Adventures and Painful Peregrinations* deserves to be read for its robust and pithy style. The title page of 1632 (pictured opposite) gives an authentic flavour.

The Totall Difcourfe,

Of the Rare Aduentures, and painefull
Peregrinations of long nineteene Yeares Tra-
uayles, from SCOTLAND, to the moft Famous
Kingdomes in *Europe*, *Afia*, and
AFFRICA.

Perfited by three deare bought Voyages,

in Surueighing of Forty eight Kingdomes ancient
and Moderne ; twenty one Rei-publickes, ten
abfolute Principalities, *with two*
hundred Ilands.

The particular Names whereof, are Defcribed
in each Argument of the ten Diuifions of this
HISTORY : And it alfo diuided in
Three Bookes ; two whereof, ne-
uer heretofore Publifhed.

Wherein is Contayned, an exaɛt Relation, of the
Lawes, Religion, Policies, and Gouernment of all
their Princes, Potentates, and People.

Together with the grieuous Tortures he fuffered, by the
Inquifition of *Malaga* in SPAINE, his
miraculous *Difcouery* and *Deliuery*
thence : And of his laft and late
Returne from the *Northerne Iles*

Cælum non Animum.

BY WILLIAM LITHGOVV.

Imprinted at *London* by *Nicholas Okes*, and are to be fold by
Nicholas Fuffell and *Humphery Mofley* at their fhops in
Pauls Church yard, at the Ball, and the white
Lyon. 1632.

Language itself has become an expansive means of escape from narrow views of Scotland and its place in the world.

Through the 1600s, Scottish poets continued to write in Gaelic, Scots, English, like William Drummond, and Latin, like George Buchanan. Another fine poet of place was the Latinist Arthur Johnston, whose poems have been recently translated by the contemporary poet, Robert Crawford. Johnston takes an elevated view of Edinburgh, who rises on her rock 'so she can see directly into heaven'. 'A palace,' enthuses Johnson, 'glints just below Arthur's Seat,' while the castle rules over the city like Jove and the High Kirk of St Giles beams out a message of faith above the law courts. James in London, please take note!

> The Tiber frightens Rome, the sea scares Venice,
> But Edinburgh smiles at all such fuss.
> Believe me, nowhere more deserves a sceptre,
> No town on earth's more suited to command.[2]

Another ornament of this hidden Enlightenment in the 17th century was the poet and orientalist George Strachan. He was the first to translate from Farsi and Arabic, but his work remains under the radar in European archives. A devout Roman Catholic, Strachan spent most of his life in exile. At home in Scotland, religion remained the all-consuming issue.

Religion in Retreat

Charles I succeeded his father in 1625. He lacked James' nous and his savvy about Scotland but had thoroughly imbibed the old King's doctrines of their divine right to rule. He proceeded to impose Anglican-style church government and worship on the Scots Presbyterians with predictable results. In 1637 the introduction of a set liturgy from *The Book of Common Prayer* provoked a riot in St Giles Church, during which the legendary Jenny Geddes hurled her stool at the minister, shouting 'daur ye say mass in my lug (ear)?'

In 1638 the National Covenant was signed in Greyfriars Church in defence of the idea that the nation had a special covenant with God to uphold true, ie Presbyterian, religion. But important as this righteous indignation was, it was driven by a revolt against government from London. Those different emphases were in due course to split apart, leading to internal conflicts in addition to the war with English authority. By 1639, armed conflict had broken out in Scotland, England and Ireland. One oppressive regime followed another in Edinburgh, including a period in the 1650s when Oliver Cromwell abolished Scotland in favour of his personal 'Commonwealth'.

Strange to say, one of the main victims of this extended and increasingly rancid conflict was religion. As William Drummond wrote, framing his words historically as if addressed to James IV,

It is to be wished that the onlie true Religion were in the heartes of all your Subjectes. Since diversitie of opinions of Religione and heresies, are the verie punishment of God almightie upon men for their horrible vices and roring Sinnes. And when Men forsake his feare and true obedience, God abandoneth them to their own opinions and fantasies in Religion: out of which arise partialities, factions, divisions, strife, intestine discords, which burst forthe into civil warres, and in short time bring Kingdomes and Commonwealthes to their laste Periodes.

This address on Toleration was left unpublished, as Drummond abandoned his History of Scotland in the face of exactly such open conflict, with repression on all fronts. Tolerance and dialogue were firmly in retreat.

Yet, setting aside the blast and counter-blast of religious controversy, Scottish writers of all kinds continued to express their own varieties of religious experience. Amongst them were some distinguished women poets, such as Sìleas MacDonald (Sìleas na Ceapaich), whose Gaelic Hymn on the loss of both her husband and her daughter ends with this brave stanza.

> Glory to the Son of Mary
> Who gave me the gift of suffering pain,
> And so much grief and sadness
> That my blood and flesh have left me,
> Until my Saviour will come
> Restoring me to life once more;
> On that day, lift up my soul,
> O King, to the citadel of Music.

> Glòir thoir do Mhac Muire
> Thug e ghibht domh gun d'fhuiling mi leòn,
> Thug de bhròn's de leann-dubh dhomh
> Gus na theirig de m'fhuil agus m'fheòil.
> Gus an tigeadh mo Shlànair
> A rithisd 'gam shàbhaladh beò;
> Rìgh, glac m'anam an latha ud
> 'S thoir suas e gu Cathair a' Cheòil.

Nurtured, by contrast, in a strongly Protestant tradition, Elizabeth Melville takes up a similar melody of suffering and hope.

> My dear brother, with courage beare the crosse,
> Joy shall be joined with all thy sorrow here;
> High is thy hope; disdaine this earthly drosse!
> ....
> Look to the Lord, thou art not left alone,
> Since he is here, what pleasure canst thou take!
> He is at hand and hears thy heavy moan,
> End out thy faucht, and suffer for his sake!
> A sight most bright thy sould shall shortly see,
> When store of glore they rich reward shall be.

In this case, though, the brother is a metaphoric 'brother in Christ', a Presbyterian minister imprisoned in Blackness Castle, rather than an actual family member. Elizabeth Melville lived just over the Forth at Culross.

The power of poetry to express collective religious emotion had been recognised in the 16th century Reformation through the creation of *Gude and Godly Ballatis*, which were sung communally like folk songs to popular secular melodies. This stream was strengthened in the Presbyterian tradition through the singing of metrical psalms in unison. Many of these settings, such as Psalm 23 'The Lord's my Shepherd', continue to be sung today. Later, Gaelic psalm singing emerged with a precentor giving out the first line, and members of the congregation responding with variations and ornamentation. This is now recognised as a musical genre in its own right. Metrical paraphrases of other Biblical texts expanded the repertoire.

The puritan preachers were not all arid controversialists. Some previously unknown poems by Elizabeth Melville were recently discovered on a manuscript of sermons by Robert Bruce, Minister of St Giles Church. His reflections on the New Testament's Letter to the Hebrews had inspired Melville to take up the same theme of faith as the great enduring constant. Bruce was also the author of a published series of sermons on 'the Mystery of the Lord's Supper', which are often mentioned by historians, though less often read. Admiration of these spiritual reflections must, however, be tempered by the knowledge that Robert Bruce played a significant role in the torture and execution of women accused of witchcraft. This draconian power had been handed by James VI to the Presbyterian Kirk in order to sweeten the bitter pill of re-imposing bishops.

It is hard not to conclude that women were left worse off after the Protestant Reformation, which enforced patriarchy more strictly and systematically than in medieval times. Edinburgh's prosperity as a trading burgh was to give women more scope as traders and merchants, but they were long excluded in the new dispensation from medicine, the law and religious office. The cruel persecution of folk healers and others as 'witches' in the 17th century is an enduring stain on Scotland's reputation.

Samuel Rutherford and, later, Thomas Boston were Puritan divines who dealt in learned theology and controversy. But they also produced letters and memoirs revealing a yearning for other spiritual realms, such as this 'Rhapsodical Meditation' of Rutherford:

There is not a rose out of heaven, but there is a blot and a
thorn growing out of it, except that only rose of Sharon, which

blossometh out of glory. Every leaf of that rose is a heaven, and serveth 'for the healing of the nations'; every white and red in it, is incomparable glory; every act of breathing out its smell, from everlasting to everlasting, is spotless and unmixed happiness.

This inner spirituality is also expressed by the contemplative Henry Scougal and the Quaker Robert Barclay. But it was hard to hear such voices amidst the din of controversy and the clash of weapons.

Towards the end of the hard 17th century, Robert Kirk, the minister of Balquhidder and then Aberfoyle, penned a remarkable treatise, *The Secret Commonwealth of Elves, Fauns and Fairies*. His book is an early form of religious anthropology based on a spiritual philosophy of nature. It deals with fairy lore, second sight and other perceptions of the supernatural. By bringing understanding to bear on these phenomena, Kirk undermines accusations of demonic witchcraft and points towards the Scottish Enlightenment. Kirk also acquired Gaelic and made the first translation of the Bible into Scottish Gaelic. According to legend, Robert Kirk was abducted by 'the little people' for divulging too many of their secrets, but his orderly tomb can still be seen in Aberfoyle kirkyard, close by the Fairy Hill on which he is supposed to have vanished.

Kingdoms of the Word

Over all, Scotland's 17th-century literary honours lie more with the Royalists than Calvinist Presbyterians. The Covenanters' political leader Archibald Campbell, Marquis of Argyll, was a formidable operative who deployed the language of deceit as a deadly weapon against his foes. The Royalist leader, James Graham, Marquis of Montrose, who had originally signed the Covenant as a national cause, proved to be a poet.

These verses from 'My Dear and Only Love', Graham's love tribute to his wife, Magdalen Carnegie, is much anthologised.

> My dear and only love I pray
> This noble world of thée
> Be govern'd by no other sway
> But purest monarchy.
> For if confusion have a part,
> Which virtuous souls abhor,
> And hold a synod in thy heart,
> I'll never love thee more.
>
> Like Alexander I will reign,
> And I will reign alone,
> My thoughts should evermore disdain
> A rival on my throne.
> He either fears his fate too much,
> Or his deserts are small,
> That puts it not unto the touch
> To win or lose it all.

In politics and war, Montrose did 'put it unto the touch' without the martial bravura of his Highland supporters such as the bard Iain Lòm MacDonald, who exulted over the bloody defeat of Argyll at Inverlochy. Betrayed and sentenced to death, like William Wallace before him, Montrose displayed his own form of mastery.

> Let them bestow on ev'ry airth a limb;
> Open all my veins that I may swim
> To thee my Saviour, in that Crimson Lake;
> Then place my purboil'd Head upon a Stake;
> Scatter my ashes, throw them in the Air:
> Lord (since Thou know'st where all these Atoms are)
> I'm hopeful, once, Thou'lt recollect my Dust,
> And confident Thou'lt raise me with the Just.

Again, there is an uncanny foreshadowing in these lines. James Graham was executed and dismembered in 1650, which seemed the lowest point in Royalist fortunes. But ten years later his mortal remains were re-assembled at Holyrood Palace and taken in a state funeral procession for burial in St Giles Church. The Marquis of Argyll was tried and executed, and his head was placed on the same stake by which his arch enemy Montrose had been impaled. Today, the rivals remain interred in chapels on opposing sides of St Giles Cathedral.

Royalism found dignified eloquence in James Graham's poetry, yet it also birthed anarchic defiance in the prose of Sir Thomas Urquhart of Cromarty. Imprisoned after the Scots defeat at Worcester in 1561 (attempting to restore Charles II and his crown), Urquhart penned a chaotically multiform treatise called *The Jewel*. This was intended to demonstrate his exceptional worth and so win his release. The full pseudo-learned title means gold in a dunghill, or as the author expatiates:

ΕΚΣΚΥΒΑΛΑΥΡΟΝ':

OR,

The Discovery of

A most exquisite JEWEL,

more precious then Diamonds
inchased in Gold, the like whereof
was never seen in any age; found in the
kennel of *Worcester*-streets, the day
after the Fight, and six before the Au-
tumnal Æquinox, *anno* 1651.

Serving in this place,

To frontal a VINDICATION

of the honour of *SCOTLAND,*
from that Infamy, whereinto the Rigid
Presbyterian party of that Nation,
out of their Covetousness and
ambition, most dissembled-
ly hath involved it.

Distichon ad Librum sequitur, quo tres ter adæquant
Musarum numerum, casus, & articuli.

voc.   nom.   1 abl.   2 abl.   dat.
O thou'rt a Book in truth with love to many,
    3 abl.   4 abl. acc.   gen.
Done by and for the free'st-spoke *Scot* of any.

Efficiens & finis sunt sibi invicem causæ.

LONDON, Printed by *Ja: Cottrel*; and are to
be sold by *Rich. Baddely*, at the Middle-
Temple-gate. 1652.

The treatise is also an introduction to Urquhart's proposal to construct a Universal Language, building on his already proven mathematical ingenuity. Those proofs, however, had been unfortunately lost in the aftermath of the battle. Memorably, *The Jewel* also contains extended praise of 'The Admirable Crichton' who was celebrated, according to Urquhart, across Europe as the exemplar of Scots eloquence and wisdom, and as a rebuke to the Puritan nobodies. In this encomiastic flow, Crichton and Urquhart seem to blend into the same triumphant archetype of native genius.

Despite the hyperbole, Urquhart's work emits flashes of insight from a steady flow of linguistic invention. This was proven in exile, when the now dispossessed Laird of Cromarty translated the first two books of Rabelais' *Gargantua and Pantagruel* into Scots English. Urquhart's rendering is a glorious response to one of Europe's most prized humanist authors. Where Rabelais deploys 20 adjectives, Urquhart piles on at least 30. If Rabelais delivers runs of a dozen vituperative insults, Urquhart doubles the score. The Laird matches his original in wit and ribald rhetoric. Quotation is inadequate, but sample the commentary of young Gargantua's nurse on his penis.

> But hearken, good fellows, the spigot ill betake you, and
> whirl round your brains, if you do not give ear! This little
> lecher was always groping his nurses and governesses, upside
> down, arsiversy, topsyturvy, harri bourriquet, with a Yacco
> haick, hyck gio! handling them very rudely in jumbling
> and tumbling them to keep them going; for he had already
> begun to exercise the tools, and put his codpiece in practice.

Which codpiece, or braguette, his governesses did every day
deck up and adorn with fair nosegays, curious rubies, sweet
flowers, and fine silken tufts, and very pleasantly would pass
their time in taking you know what between their fingers,
and dandling it, till it did revive and creep up to the bulk
and stiffness of a suppository, or street magdaleon, which
is a hard rolled-up salve spread upon leather. Then did they
burst out in laughing, when they saw it lift up its ears, as
if the sport had liked them. One of them would call it her
little dille, her staff of love, her quillety, her faucetin, her
dandilolly. Another, her peen, her jolly kyle, her bableret, her
membretoon, her quickset imp: another again, her branch of
coral, her female adamant, her placket-racket, her Cyprian
sceptre, her jewel for ladies. And some of the other women
would give it these names – my bunguetee, my stopple too,
my bush-rusher, my gallant wimble, my pretty borer, my
coney-burrow-ferret, my little piercer, my augretine, my
dangling hangers, down right to it, stiff and stout, in and to,
my pusher, dresser, pouting stick, my honey pipe, my pretty
pillicock, linky pinky, futilletie, my lusty andouille, and
crimson chitterling, my little couille bredouille, my pretty
rogue, and so forth.

Unfortunately Urquhart did not finish his translation, but
died in exile at Middleburg, the Scots staple port in Holland.
Reputedly, he expired from excessive laughter after hearing that
Charles II was being restored to his throne.

It is tempting to classify Thomas Urquhart as an uproarious
one-off, but that would be a mistake. He belongs in a tradi-

tion of Scots translation, and also exemplifies a vein of fantastic imagination and exuberant invention that sits alongside Scottish Literature's social and psychological realism. In Urquhart's lifetime, Cyrano de Bergerac was doing for French literature what the Laird was doing for Scotland, while adding science fiction to the mix. All of this was later to influence Alasdair Gray, AL Kennedy and Edwin Morgan in the 20th century. Morgan provided an exuberant and hugely successful Scots adaptation of Edmond de Rostand's *Cyrano de Bergerac* for Communicado Theatre.

Urquhart's achievement also flags the growing importance of prose in Scottish literature. Early in the 17th century, John Barclay published inventive prose Romances in Latin, and has some claim to being the first Scottish novelist. In 1660, the prominent lawyer Sir George Mackenzie produced *Aretina*, another classical Romance and the first Scottish novel in English. Neither writer, however, comes near Urquhart's zestful if prolific originality.

At the same time, Mackenzie was gearing up for suppression of the Covenanters, as the Royalist side resumed government in Scotland. He was to earn the descriptor 'Bluidy Mackenzie'. It was to take another 150 years before Scotland's novelists seriously faced up to the bitter legacy of these 'Killing Times'.

Comedy Is No Show

Despite George Buchanan's playwriting legacy, the 17th century had little to offer Scotland in the way of theatre. A neoclassical comedy, *Philotus*, penned by Anonymous, was published in Edinburgh in 1603 but not performed until the 20th century.

Following the Restoration in 1660, the brave or foolhardy Thomas Sydserf opened a theatre in the Canongate, but he was beaten up for his pains and his plays had to find favour in London. Charles II sent his brother James to govern Scotland and he encouraged some private theatre performances at the palace. Otherwise, the soil was barren.

As the century waned, the 'Glorious Revolution' overthrew James VII and II, who had succeeded Charles with the same kind of success as his father, Charles I, had achieved in succeeding his grandfather, James VI and I. The resistance in Scotland was led by John Graham, acclaimed as Bonnie Dundee, who won a major victory at Killiecrankie at the cost of his own life. This rising marks the beginning of the Jacobite movement in Scotland, which was to have huge cultural influence far beyond any realistic recall of the exiled and Roman Catholic Stuart line.

The new Presbyterian establishment in Edinburgh did, however, provoke a satiric drama co-written by the learned Jacobite doctor and poet Archibald Pitcairne. Known as *The Assembly* or *The Phanaticks*, this play uses the form of a Restoration comedy to pillory the Puritans as power-hungry and licentious hypocrites. Since there was no public theatre in Edinburgh, the play may have circulated in manuscript for private reading, like Russian samizdat literature. So Scottish writing ended the century as it had begun, providing a form of cultural resistance, struggling to keep Scotland in the European mainstream. In the words of Pitcairne's defiant prologue,

> It's a long whyle since any play hath been
> Except rope dancing in oure nation seen

> Our northern cuntre seldom tastes of witt.
> Our too cold Clime is justlie blamed for itt.
> Nothing our hearts can move, our fancie bribe
> Except the gibberish of the canting tribe.
> ....
> Yet if this play but tack, we'al promise more,
> For of this kinde we have laide up ane stoir,
> Matter enough to mack at least a scoir.

And at the close an explicitly Jacobite pitch.

> And now since prayers are so much in vogue,
> We will with an candle our epilogue.
> Let the just heavns our king and peace restore,
> And villains never wrong us anymore.

Perhaps in its own way that was a pious hope.

147

SEVEN

The 18th Century:
Philosophers, Poets and Patriots

Capital Without a Nation?

IN HINDSIGHT, THE period between the 'Glorious Revolution' of 1688–9 and the Scottish parliament disbanding in 1707 looks like an interlude. Once again a constitutional settlement, based this time on Scotland's Presbyterian Claim of Right, failed to settle anything.

Initially, the point was to retrospectively tidy up the mess left by James VII and II's precipitate flight. His overthrow was wrapped up into the accession of James' daughter Mary and her husband William (both II in Scotland), inaugurating a new era of constitutional monarchy. The powers of the Scottish Parliament were augmented and, wearied by religious wrangling, William ceded an ecclesiastical monopoly to the Presbyterian Kirk. In reality, William had little interest in Scotland, and was focused on European wars and securing finance for them from the English parliament.

Scotland continued to be excluded from England's imperial trade. The attempt to found a Scottish colony at Darien in the Isthmus of Panama was undermined by Spanish and English naval blockades and a hostile local environment. This emptied Scotland of cash resources, while a series of bad harvests led to disease and starvation. On the more positive side, the Scottish Parliament legislated to establish a school in every parish, finally realising John Knox's vision of universal education.

Then the succession problem again reared its head. William and Mary were childless, so they were succeeded by another of

James' daughters, Anne. Despite 17 pregnancies, none of her children survived to adulthood, the last dying in 1701. Then the heat was on to ensure that the Scottish Parliament supported England's Protestant succession by choosing Sophia, Electress of Hanover as next in line. But there was considerable support in Scotland for restoring the direct Stuart line through James VII and II's son, also James, who came to be known as the Old Pretender.

The English parliament threatened a trade embargo and confiscation of Scottish assets in London if the Scots would not conform. The battle was finally settled by offering Scotland's landed elite substantial bribes and buying off the Kirk with the promise of an Act, separate from the Treaty of Union, which would guarantee its legal status as the established Church of Scotland.

The Incorporating Union of Parliaments appeared to resolve the halfway status of Scotland under the Union of the Crowns. But the guarantees of 1707 were remarkably short lived. In 1711, Westminster's House of Lords voted to restore to Scottish landowners 'their ancient Right of presenting Ministers to the Churches vacant in that part of Great Britain called Scotland'. The 16 Scottish Peers all voted against, knowing that a congregation's right to 'call their Minister' was a foundation stone of Presbyterianism. This was followed in 1712 by an Act of the Toleration of Episcopacy in the face of furious Presbyterian opposition. But Scottish representatives in Westminster were outnumbered and ignored.

Almost immediately, secessions or splits began in the Scottish Church, as those opposing subordination to secular government in London left to set up dissident churches. Religious disputes were re-ignited, building to the crescendo of the Disruption in

1843, when a third of the Church of Scotland Ministers left to found the Free Church of Scotland. The divisive impact on education and civic life continued into the 20th century.

On a different front, the 1707 Union led immediately to a series of Jacobite Risings in favour of the exiled Stuarts. In terms of resources and support, the 1715 revolt should have succeeded, but failed through poor leadership. Despite this the Jacobite movement became strongly rooted in Scotland and culturally celebrated.

The 1689–1707 interlude was also culturally uneasy. There were signs of recovery from civil war and advances in mathematics, botany, medicine and astronomy, with major works such as James Sutherland's *Hortus Medicus Edinburgensis* sowing seeds of Enlightenment. Yet in 1697 a young Edinburgh University student, Thomas Aikenhead, was executed for questioning the existence of God. In the same period, Scots merchants aspired to trade with India and Africa, positioning themselves for a share of the lucrative traffic in human slaves. Yet the same individuals claimed Presbyterian equality and conscience as the basis of Scottish society.

The 1707 Union became a rallying point that stimulated, or galled, Scots into re-asserting their national and international distinctiveness through science, history, philosophy, poetry, art, music and even drama.

A Second Renaissance

The first important writer to articulate a fresh Renaissance was Allan Ramsay. Coming to Edinburgh from Leadhills as an apprentice wigmaker, Ramsay soon established his own wig-making business. He began to write poetry, and then transformed his business into a bookshop in the St Giles Luckenbooths, where he also added a circulating library.

Allan Ramsay's direct, vigorous poetic voice blows away the cobwebs and exudes a fresh, inclusive humanism. His early works include a celebrated 'Elegy for Maggie Johnson' the brewer.

> Auld Reeky, mourn in sable hue,
> Let fouth of tears dreep like May dew;
> To braw tippony (twopenny ale) bid adieu,
> Which we with greed
> Bended as fast as she could brew: —
> But ah! she's dead.
>
> To tell the truth now, Maggy dang (excelled),
> Of customers she had a bang (crowd);
> For lairds and souters a' did gang
> To drink bedeen (quickly):
> The barn and yard was aft sae thrang,
> We took the green;
>
> And there by dizens we lay down,
> Syne sweetly ca'd the healths around,
> To bonny lasses black or brown,
> As we loo'd best:
> In bumpers we dull cares did drown,
> And took our rest.
>
> When in our pouch we found some clinks,
> And took a turn o'er Bruntsfield Links,

> Aften in Maggy's, at hy-jinks,
> We guzzled scuds (foaming ale),
> Till we could scarce, wi' hale-out drinks,
> Cast off our duds (jackets).

In full comic vein, he poeticised the last advice of the brothel keeper Lucky Spence to her young charges. And in a heartfelt vein he elegised Lucky Wood, a popular tavern keeper in the Canongate.

> O Cannigate! poor elritch (horrible) hole,
> What loss, what crosses dost thou thole!
> London and death gar thee look drole,
> And hing thy head:
> Wow, but thou hast e'en a cauld coal
> To blaw indeed.
>
> Hear me, ye hills, and every glen,
> Ilk craig, ilk cleugh, and hollow den,
> And echo shrill, that a' may ken
> The waefou thud
> Be rackless Death, wha came unseen
> To Lucky Wood.

Alongside these urban poems, Ramsay wrote pastoral verse and epistles in the style of the Roman poet Horace. These include a verse letter penned from Mavisbank in Midlothian commiserating with a friend who is back in Edinburgh's smoke and noise, and a rich Scots 'Ode to Mr Forbes'.

Now gowans sprout and lavrocks sing,
And welcome west winds warm the spring,
O'er hill and dale they saftly blaw,
And drive the winter's cauld awa.
The ships lang gyzened (warped) at the pier
Now spread their sails and smoothly steer.
The nags and nowt (cattle) hate wissened strae,
And frisking to the fields they gae
....
With her gay train the Paphian Queen
By moonlight dances on the green;
She leads while Nymphs and Graces sing,
And trip around the fairy ring.

Ramsay was also a fine songwriter, combining classicism with the vernacular. With ease he circumvents later divides between Romanticism and Classicism which dog English Literature. To achieve this, he draws on three centuries of Scottish poetic tradition while remaining an innovator.

Using his bookshop as a creative hub, Allan Ramsay built relationships with publishers and editors, such as Thomas Ruddiman, and with fellow poets such as William Hamilton of Gilbertfield, translator of *The Wallace*. He launched a series of *Tea Table Miscellanies* offering new lyrics to traditional melodies, so reviving folksong. His *Evergreen* journal put the repertoire of the 16th century Bannatyne Manuscript back into circulation, encouraging new work in older forms such as his own poem 'The Vision'.

In addition to poetry and music, Ramsay championed the

visual arts, co-founding an Academy of St Luke in Edinburgh and supporting his own artist son, the younger Allan Ramsay, to study in Italy. For Ramsay, all of these strands came together in his love for drama and his determination to restore live theatre to Edinburgh. He expanded his popular pastoral play *The Gentle Shepherd* with songs and dances, and in 1836 he opened his own theatre in Carrubbers Close off the High Street.

This was a bridge too far for the Town Council, which had already tried and failed to close Ramsay's circulating library for, in their terms, distributing pornography. In 1837 they closed the theatre, using a recent Act of the Westminster parliament which introduced theatre licensing, but only for two theatres in London. Here was another bitter fruit of the Union which Ramsay and many of his associates deeply resented. *The Gentle Shepherd* was a Jacobite play concealed as a Restoration Romance, none of which endeared Ramsay or his works to the Presbyterian Councillors and lawyers.

Yet Allan Ramsay was determined and resilient. He remains one of the most attractive characters in Edinburgh and Scotland's literary story. His statue, topped with a wigmakers silk turban, still stands on Princes Street, overlooked by the octagonal house which he created below the Castle. It is now part of Ramsay Gardens.

Renaissance to Enlightenment

In 18th-century Scotland, history, science and philosophy all contributed to literature. As Ramsay retired to live congenially in his new house, a wave of innovation was set in motion by a group which came to be known as the Enlightenment literati. They included David Hume, philosopher and later historian; Adam Smith, moral philosopher and economist; William Robertson, historian and divine; and the social scientist Adam Ferguson. Among the leading scientists were Joseph Black, the chemist, and the geologist James Hutton who deduced the immense age of the earth from observations of the Scottish Landscape, including Salisbury Crags in Edinburgh. It is fair to say that the close friends Hume and Smith had the widest and longest-lasting influence.

Portraits of Hume in later life depict an ample, prosperous gentleman, comfortable with his fame as an essayist and historian. By this time he was settled in Edinburgh and combined his own writing with being Librarian of the Advocates Library, later to become the National Library of Scotland. But these images belie Hume's early struggles.

Born in Edinburgh to Border lairds, Hume barely made his way financially as a law student and then clerk. Instead of focussing on his employment, he consumed the widest possible range of learning and wrestled in Bristol and then France with the core principles of moral philosophy. This intensity led to some form of breakdown and also to *A Treatise of Human Nature* which, by Hume's admission, 'fell stillborn from the press'. It is now a philosophical classic, but remains a difficult read, as Hume grapples with how the senses provide human experience, and how such 'impressions' can form the basis of our ideas.

Hume's probing enquiries made him sceptical about the ultimate reliability of any human knowledge. This scepticism led to a huge philosophical backlash, led by Scottish philosopher Thomas Reid, to rebuild a common-sense basis for knowledge. The implications of Hume's scepticism for religious belief was an even hotter potato. He was denied professorships at Edinburgh and Glasgow Universities on the basis of 'atheism', when he was clearly the outstanding candidate.

Hume's mature style is balanced and mellifluous, embracing reason and sentiment or emotion.

> The end of all moral speculations is to teach us our duty; and by proper representations of the deformity of vice and beauty of virtue, beget correspondent habits, and engage us to avoid the one, and embrace the other. But is this ever expected from inferences and conclusions of the understanding, which of themselves have no hold of the affections, or set in motion the active powers of men? They discover truths; but where the truths which they discover are indifferent, and beget no desire or aversion, they can have no influence on conduct and behaviour.

What is omitted here is the strong influence of religion on the emotions, but Hume is edging religion out of the field of humane understanding.

Despite his later fame as an economist and the author of *The Wealth of Nations*, Adam Smith was grounded in moral philosophy, and he considered *The Theory of Moral Sentiment* to be his most important book. His prose style, like Hume's, avoids the rhythms of spoken Scots in favour of formal English.

> How selfish soever man may be supposed, there are evidently some principles in his nature, which interest him in the fortunes of others […] Of this kind is pity or compassion, the emotion which we feel for the misery of others, when we

either see it, or are made to conceive it in a very lively manner […] This sentiment, like all the other original passions of human nature, is by no means confined to the virtuous and humane, though they may perhaps feel it with the most exquisite sensibility. The greatest ruffian, the most hardened violator of the laws of society, is not altogether without it.

Smith also pursues political ideas.

Nothing tends so much to promote public spirit as the study of politics, of the several systems of civil government, their advantages and disadvantages, of the constitution of our own country […] its commerce, its defence, the disadvantages it labours under, the dangers to which it may be exposed, how to remove the one, and how to guard against the other. Upon this account political disquisitions, if just, and reasonable, and practicable, are of all the works of speculation the most useful […] They serve to animate the public passions of men, and rouse them to seek out the means of promoting the happiness of the society.

The tone aims to include us, the readers, in a contract of reasonableness. Smith rejects the pessimistic attitudes on which Calvinist social systems like Presbyterianism were based. Some Church of Scotland Ministers, named the Moderates, agreed with Smith and advocated an Enlightenment version of Christianity. At the same time, Smith regarded the Republican ideals of Andrew Fletcher of Saltoun, who wanted Scotland to be an independent home of freedom and virtue like ancient Sparta, as unrealistic.

Smith and Hume were not, however, lacking in national sentiment, believing that their Enlightenment intention was a patriotic project. Proud of Scotland's achievement in viewing human development and society through a historical lens, Hume boasted that 'this is the historical age and this the historical nation'.

Some of Hume's finest writing, *The Natural History of Religion* and *Dialogues Concerning Natural Religion,* could not be published in his own lifetime. He left them with Smith to decide about publication, but the moderate Smith regarded these works as too controversial for public consumption. In Smith's defence, David Hume's handsome tomb in the Calton Burial Ground had to be guarded against any righteous desecration. Yet it is not clear that Hume was an atheist, which would have been a very definite position for a sceptic. But in his writing on religion, Hume eloquently demolishes any claims to infallibility on the part of religions.

Whaur's Yir Wullie Shakespeare Noo?

Another form of cultural patriotism endorsed by the Enlightenment literati was drama, and not just the schoolroom variety. By mid-century, Edinburgh finally had its own working theatre, The Canongate Playhouse, and the literati backed one of their own, John Home the Minister of Athelstaneford in East Lothian, to revive 'the national drama'. They not only lent their prestigious support, but even attended a read-through of Home's new play *Douglas*, in which they voiced the playwright's characters, male and female, with thespian bravado, ahead of professional production.

On 14 December 1756, *Douglas* was duly premiered to a packed house in the Canongate. Advance puffs had indicated that all members of the clergy would be welcome, and that tickets could be secured from David Hume's lodgings. None of this was designed to calm the occasion, and emotions were running high.

Home's *Douglas* is a version of the traditional ballad 'Gil Morrice', a tragic tale of concealed identity, heroism, love and bloody murder. While modulating some of this for politer taste, Home spares none of the dramatic reversals and passion-laden revelations. The son of Leith's Town Clerk, Home aspires to a classical tragedy fit for the Athens of the North.

Yet Scotland's own dramas were more upfront than this might suggest. Home himself had volunteered to fight against Bonnie Prince Charlie in 1745–6. He was taken prisoner at the Battle of Falkirk, but subsequently escaped. By comparison to Scotland's recent history, which no-one in Enlightenment Edinburgh wished to recall, *Douglas* is melodramatic in treatment and stilted in language.

> *Enter Douglas with a sword in each hand.*
> DOUGLAS: My mother's voice!
> I can protect thee still.
> LADY RANDOLPH: He lives, he lives:
> For this, for this to heav'n eternal praise!
> But sure I saw thee fall.
> DOUGLAS: It was Glenalvon.
> Just as my arm had master'd Randolph's sword,
> The villain came behind me: but I slew him.
> LADY RANDOLPH: Behind thee! Ah – thou'rt wounded!
> O my child,
> How pale thou lookst! and shall I lose thee now?

DOUGLAS. Do not despair: I feel a little faintness;
I hope it will not last.
Leans upon his sword.
LADY RANDOLPH: There is no hope!
And We must part! the hand of death is on thee!
O my beloved child! O Douglas, Douglas!
Douglas growing more and more faint.
DOUGLAS: Too soon we part: I have not long been
Douglas.
O destiny! hardly thou deal'st with me:
Clouded and hid, a stranger to myself,
In low and poor obscurity I liv'd.
LADY RANDOLPH: Has heav'n preserv'd thee for an
end like this?
DOUGLAS: O had I fallen as my brave fathers fell,
Turning with great effort the tide of battle! [...]
LADY RANDOLPH: Hear justice! hear! Stretch thy
avenging arm.
Douglas falls.
DOUGLAS: Unknown I die; no tongue shall speak of me.
Some noble spirits, judging by themselves,
May yet conjecture what 1 might have prov'd,
And think life only wanting to my fame:
But who shall comfort thee?
LADY RANDOLPH: Despair! despair!
DOUGLAS: O had it pleas'd high heav'n to let me live
A little while! My eyes that gaze on thee
Grow dim apace! my mother – Oh! my mother!
Dies.

On the night, the audience received this with rapture, and one spontaneous heckler cried out 'Whaur's yir Wullie Shakespeare noo!', though some have argued it was 'Whaur's yir Wullie noo?'. Unfortunately this unintentionally nails the play's fundamental weakness – the lack of vernacular Scots idiom.

As a consequence of the night's reverberations, John Home resigned as a clergyman, while some of his colleagues were publicly rebuked by the Church for attending. Home wrote for the London stage without long-term success, but continued as a respected Enlightenment figure, becoming Tutor to the Prince of Wales, a founder of the Royal Society of Edinburgh and a local MP. The national drama was once more postponed.

Identity Dramas

The temporary occupation of Edinburgh (minus the Castle) by Bonnie Prince Charlie in 1745 had little long-term impact on the capital's fabric or politics. A majority remained loyal to the Hanoverian monarchs in London, while a minority were Jacobites. Across the rest of Scotland, it was the other way round for at least another decade. The Jacobite victories at Prestonpans in East Lothian and at Falkirk inspired poetry on both sides of the divide, while the Battle of Culloden was widely lamented due to its aftermath of ethnic cleansing and cultural repression.

James Macpherson's *Poems of Ossian* was a deeply meditated response to the Jacobite Rising and the suppression of Gaeldom. Macpherson, who grew up near Kingussie in the shadow of the Ruthven Barracks, experienced this at first hand. He claimed his first poems as fragments of a Gaelic epic cycle which might be

THE I8TH CENTURY: PHILOSOPHERS, POETS AND PATRIOTS

equivalent to Homer. He had studied the Greek bard at Aberdeen University under Thomas Blackwell, who was the first scholar to understand that Homer arose from an oral tradition. However, though Macpherson's Gaelic sources were genuine and abundant, there was no overarching epic.

Controversy ensued. Hugh Blair, Edinburgh's Enlightenment Professor of Rhetoric and Belles Lettres, was a passionate advocate for Ossian. For a time Macpherson lived below Blair in Edinburgh's Blackfriars Street, sharing the 'translations' or recreations of Ossian with his mentor as he wrote. But Dr Johnson, London's authoritative man of letters, led an attack on Ossian's authenticity, charging Macpherson with 'fraud'. Macpherson himself was driven into claiming too much, yet the prosecution case failed to acknowledge the evidence for extensive knowledge of Ossian songs and stories in oral tradition.

The Poems of Ossian became an international sensation and an icon of Romanticism championed by, among many, Thomas Jefferson and Napoleon, who slept with Ossian under his pillow. From now on, literature in Scotland had to deal with the nation's disproportionate role in Romantic perceptions. At the same time, Scottish writers were far from finished with Jacobite enthusiasm.

These dramas featured on historical, theatrical and pictorial stages, but they also fed an inner theatre of identity. This fermented with exceptional vigour in the fertile imagination of James Boswell. Later nicknamed Bozzie, James was brought up mainly in Edinburgh because his father, the Laird of Auchinleck in Ayrshire, was a prominent advocate and then High Court judge. By his own account, Boswell shone as a young student of languages at Edinburgh University, but then made an unscheduled bolt for freedom in London. This was a typically full-on Bozzie reaction to his father's austere scholarship, Presbyterian religion and, above all, sexual repression.

James had to be fetched home, but Lord Auchinleck decided that an authorised period in London, followed by some travel in Europe in the tradition of a grand tour, might settle his son and heir into the legal career which had been mapped out for him. Never was a more explosive Pandora's Box opened by a concerned yet well-meaning parent.

James Boswell's travels, his door-stepping of 'great men', his profligate sex life, his depressions and drinking bouts add up to something remarkable by any measure; but what made them unique was Bozzie's compulsion to record every possible moment in astoundingly frank, confessional journals. And, against all the odds, the journals, squirrelled away by relatives and then forgotten, survived into modern times.

Reading the journals, it seems Boswell himself could not be convinced he had actually had these experiences until he recorded and dramatised them. He needed this validation of his own existence. 'I should live no more than I can record,' he stated, and then, as if in baffled wonder at his own contradictions, 'It's amazing how very different I am at different times.'

Paradoxically, despite his life of incorrigible attention seeking, the Journal had to be kept secret. But Boswell compensated for this by circulating some of the material in private letters and by becoming a publicity junkie, writing about himself anonymously in the press and staging PR stunts like his appearance in costume as 'Corsica Boswell', champion of the cause of Corsican independence led by General Paolozzi, whom he had pursued across the island during his European travels.

The highlight of the early journals is Boswell's time in London. Of Tuesday 18 January 1763 he records 'a little heat in the members of my body sacred to Cupid'. He shrugs this aside, however, having only been recently with one woman. 'When I came to Louisa's I felt myself stout and well, and most courageously did I plunge into the fount of love'. The ardent lover commends Louisa as an actress who had played many fine parts, while typically stating 'how remarkably fond she was of me today'.

However, by the next day, 'too, too plain was Signor Gonorrhea'. Typically again, Bozzie blames Louisa, and gives a blow by blow account of their confrontation.

> BOSWELL: By God, Madam, I have been with none but you, and here am I very bad.
> LOUISA: Well, sir, by the same solemn oath I protest I was ignorant of it.[3]

Boswell ripostes that he would like to believe it, but 'I own on this occasion I can't believe a miracle.' It is, however, almost miraculous that we are able to read this the unpublishable first-hand account.

It was on the same extended London visit that James Boswell met Dr Johnson who was to become a substitute father for Bozzie and a vital literary collaborator. In Boswell's account, he had to own up – reluctantly – to coming from Scotland. 'But I can't help it,' he protested. 'That, I find, is what a very great many of your countrymen cannot help,' replied Johnson. Boswell's industrious mining of Johnson's conversation became the basis of his monumental biography of the sage. The *Life of Samuel Johnson* was

Bozzie's main claim to literary fame until the Journals were rediscovered and published in the 20th century.

Despite his travels and eventual relocation to London, Edinburgh continued to be central to Boswell's life and career.
Knowing that David Hume was seriously ill, Boswell went to visit
him one Sunday morning to see if the prospect of death might
have softened the philosopher's views on religion. He found poor
Hume stretched out on a sofa, looking 'lean and ghastly'. He was
wearing a scratch wig and seemed 'quite different from the plump
figure he used to present'.

But Boswell found Hume metaphysically unperturbed, so
the focus switches back on Boswell himself, and the challenge
presented to his own faith by a man of 'such strong abilities and
extensive enquiry dying in the persuasion of being annihilated'.
Then, in characteristic contradiction, Boswell acknowledges that
in Hume's pleasant company 'death did not seem so dismal'.

This seems an unpardonably insensitive intrusion. And had
Hume shown nervousness or fear, Bozzie would have spread gossip
over the town! According to Boswell, Hume was enjoying the visit,
but what did he think when the door closed behind him? We do not
know because Hume's autobiography, 'My Own Life', stretches to
two phlegmatic pages. Yet Hume's reflections on identity in his *A
Treatise of Human Nature* could apply neatly to the problems
James Boswell confronts in his Journals.

> For my part, when I enter most intimately into what I call
> myself, I always stumble on some particular perception or
> other, of hotter, cold, light or shade, love or hatred, pain
> or pleasure. I never can catch myself at any time without

a perception, and never can observe any thing but the perception.

A high point for all readers of Boswell's Journals is Dr Johnson's long planned tour of Scotland. This resulted in a bi-focal travel classic, in which we can sample Johnson's *Journey to the Western Isles of Scotland* and Boswell's parallel *Journal of a Tour to the Hebrides*. It all, however, begins in Edinburgh, as recorded in the fuller private Journal, much of which also features later in the *Life of Samuel Johnson*. James was over the moon, striding up the High Street arm-in-arm with his mentor, showing the great man the sights and introducing him to the literati.

Boswell exudes sentimental pride in Scotland. Johnson is having none of it, while sometimes showing genuine interest in aspects of Scotland's history and culture, especially the Highlands and the Jacobites. At other points it feels like Bozzie, the Scotch terrier, goading Johnson's bear into anti-Scottish swipes of the paw. This Grand Tour ends at Auchinleck, where Johnson and Boswell senior had a furious row about Charles I and Oliver Cromwell. This was more High Tory against Presbyterian Whig than England versus Scotland, but the whole business was enmeshed in the relationship between the two nations. Johnson was a passionate admirer of Mary Queen of Scots and a Jacobite, while Auchinleck was with George Buchanan on the Mary question and a resolute Hanoverian.

It is hard to sum up James Boswell. *The Diary of Samuel Pepys* contains a million words written over a decade. You have to multiply by at least five to sense Boswell's scale. World literature owes a great debt to Yale University for assembling an unsurpassed

Boswell archive and publishing widely from it. Boswell is a rule-breaking innovator of international status. Not until James Joyce in the 20th century can you name a comparable figure. Yet he belongs to Edinburgh and Scotland.

Most significantly, Boswell is irresistibly readable. There is something so simultaneously pathetic and engaging about his persona that reading his prose is almost as compulsive as it must have been to write. As he commented early on to the Journal,

> For really, to speak seriously, I think there is a blossom about me of something more distinguished than the generality of mankind. But I am much afraid that this blossom will never swell into fruit, but will be nipped and destroyed by many a blighting heat and chilling frost.

Boswell's self-conflicted humanity becomes ours as we read. We touch the oddity, the uniqueness of being alive and conscious. Robert Louis Stevenson advised taking 'a little Boswell daily', and I have found that a reliable prescription.

The Fergusson Tragedy

Unfortunately, there was no prescription available to protect Robert Fergusson from injury, insanity, poverty and death in Edinburgh's Bedlam in 1774. Yet despite his tragically early departure, aged 24, Fergusson had made his mark as an authentic laureate of Edinburgh, combining, like Ramsay, the classical and the vernacular with accomplished versatility.

A lowly clerk and frequenter of the town's taverns, races and festivals, Fergusson moved in a different social milieu from that of James Boswell. Yet, on the strength of his democratic education at St Andrews, the young poet had no hesitation in challenging Dr Johnson as an equal and criticising the fawning welcome afforded him by the University professors. Like Robert Burns, Fergusson was an opponent of the English Union and its consequences for Scottish culture and identity.

> On Scotia's plains, in days of yore,
> When lads and lasses tartan wore,
> Saft music rang on ilka shore,
> In hamely weid (garb);
> But harmony is now no more,
> And music dead.

Fergusson is reputed to have been a fine singer and his poetic metrics, as in 'Caller Oysters', evidence a good ear, measuring classical form against vigorous Scots rhythms.

> O a' the waters that can hobble (move)
> A fishing yole or sa'mon coble,
> An' can reward the fisher's trouble,
> Or south or north,
> There's nane sae spacious an' sae noble
> As Firth o' Forth.
>
> In her the skate an' codlin sail,
> The eel fu' souple wags her tail,
> Wi' herrin, fleuk, and mackarel,

An' whitins dainty:
Their spindle-shanks the labsters trail,
Wi' partans (crabs) plenty.
Auld Reikie's sons blyth faces wear;
September's merry month is near,
That brings in Neptune's caller (cool) cheer,
New oysters fresh;
The halesomest and nicest gear
O' fish or flesh.

Edinburgh features vividly in Fergusson's verse between sea and land, and through the changing seasons.

Now mirk December's dowie face
Glowrs owr the rigs wi sour grimace,
While, thro' his minimum of space,
The bleer-ey'd sun,
Wi blinkin light and stealing pace,
His race doth run.

From naked groves nae birdie sings,
To shepherd's pipe nae hillock rings,
The breeze nae od'rous flavour brings
From Borean cave,
And dwyning nature droops her wings,
Wi visage grave.

But even Edinburgh's harshest seasons bring an appropriate festive response.

Auld Reikie! thou'rt the canty hole,
A bield (shelter) for many caldrife soul,
Wha snugly at thine ingle loll,
Baith warm and couth,
While round they gar the bicker (drinking cup) roll
To weet their mouth.

When merry Yule-day comes, I trou,
You'll scantlins find a hungry mou;
Sma are our cares, our stamacks fou
O' gusty gear,
And kickshaws (novelties), strangers to our view,
Sin fairn-year.

Ye browster (brewer) wives, now busk (dress) ye
   braw,
And fling your sorrows far awa;
Then come and gie's the tither blaw
Of reaming ale,
Mair precious than the well of Spa,
Our hearts to heal

....

Fidlers, your pins in temper fix,
And roset weel your fiddle-sticks;
But banish vile Italian tricks
Frae out your quorum,
Not fortes wi pianos mix –
Gie's *Tulloch Gorum* (Scots tune).

For nought can cheer the heart sae weel
As can a canty Highland reel;
It even vivifies the heel
To skip and dance:
Lifeless is he wha canna feel
It's influence.

Some of Fergusson's festival poems pick up on the earlier tradition of folk celebration in works such as 'Christis Kirk in the Green'. But Fergusson's invention includes giving voice to the streets and kirkyards of Auld Reikie, as he heads out to the Meadows or the Royal Park in his 'gude braid claith'. It seems fitting that the poet's main monument in Edinburgh, a sculpture by David Annand, shows Fergusson nattily dressed and pigtailed, striding out of Canongate Kirkyard where he is buried, book under arm.

The city continues to have a warm affection for the poet who regarded it as his ideal audience.

Let mirth abound, let social cheer
Invest the dawning of the year;
Let blithesome innocence appear
To crown our joy;
Nor envy wi sarcastic sneer
Our bliss destroy.

And thou, great god of Aqua Vitae!
Wha sways the empire of this city,
When fou we're sometimes capernoity,
Be thou prepar'd

> To hedge us frae that black banditti,
> The City Guard.

Robert Fergusson's personal 'hail and farewell' were all for Edinburgh.

> Auld Reikie! Wale (choice) o ilka toun
> That Scotland kens beneath the moon.

And 'I ne'er could part / wi thee but wi' a dowie heart.' Somehow the feeling remains mutual.

Agnes Maclehose in Edinburgh

Robert Burns arrived in Edinburgh soon after Fergusson's death. The runaway success of the Kilmarnock Edition of his poems saved Burns from taking ship to Jamaica, where he would have worked directly or indirectly for Scots owners of the Slave Plantations. Instead, he came hotfoot to the capital in search of fame and fortune, but the first thing he wanted to do was pay his respects to Robert Fergusson, his 'elder brother in the Muse'. It was Fergusson who had inspired Burns to write in Scots and align with Scottish literary tradition. He soon learned that his hero was in an unmarked pauper's grave in Canongate Kirkyard, and at his own expense Burns ordered an inscribed tombstone, which is still there due to some later restoration work funded by Robert Louis Stevenson.

Hailed by the Freemasons as 'Caledonia's Bard', Robert Burns did find fame in Edinburgh, but no fortune. He also used Edinburgh as a base from which to tour other parts of Scotland, including the Highlands, expanding his identity as a national poet. Burns belongs more to Ayrshire and Dumfries than Edinburgh, yet some very important things came out of his capital city sojourn.

Firstly, Burns met the self-effacing James Johnson whose *Scots Musical Museum* was devoted to continuing Scots folksong in print and performance. Caledonia's Bard enthusiastically joined the cause without pay; a passion to recover and mend Scots songs drove Burns' creative passion for the rest of his life, ensuring him a place of honour in the national music of Scotland as well as its literature.

It was also in Edinburgh that Burns eventually secured a job as an Excise Officer, and was able to return home to set up house with Jean Armour and their surviving children. It is possible that this job was given to Burns in order to keep tabs on the radical poet and minimise his contact with the politics of London or Edinburgh. If so, this was only partially successful. However, some of Burns' most political poems were published anonymously. 'Scots Wha Hae' was disguised in historical garb, supposedly summarising Bruce's address before the Battle of Bannockburn, but actually directed at the treatment of Thomas Muir and 'The Democracy Martyrs' now commemorated in Calton Burial Ground.

It is interesting that Burns left Edinburgh quite suddenly after Deacon Brodie's abortive robbery of the Excise Office in Chessel's Court. Burns had been in that office a few times in pursuit of his job application. Did he worry that some of his lowlife connections in Edinburgh might put him under suspicion? Like Deacon Brodie, respectable citizen by day and burglar and gambler by night, Burns had experienced the darker sides of city life as well as its respectability and patronising snobbery. In due course, Robert Louis Stevenson would take up this theme of Edinburgh's double life.

On another front, Burns experienced professional theatre in Edinburgh, becoming friendly with the actors of the Theatre Royal. Like Allan Ramsay before him, Burns felt that drama was an essential part of the national poetic endeavour. But his uncertain status as the son of a poor tenant farmer excluded him from writing for the Edinburgh stage. As his masterpiece 'Tam o' Shanter' and his ballad folk opera 'Love and Liberty' demonstrate, Burns had the requisite gifts. The capital's snobbery became Scotland's loss. Perhaps acknowledging this, Thomas Hamilton's design for the Burns Monument on Calton Hill is crowned with a Greek tripod, which was awarded to Aeschylus, Sophocles and Euripides as winning dramatists in the Athenian theatre festival.

Similar dualities dogged Robert Burns' romantic friendship with Nancy Maclehose, better known as Clarinda to the poet's Sylvander. This complex and likely unconsummated relationship was conducted through an extended and intense 'pastoral' correspondence, punctuated with passionate encounters. On leaving Edinburgh, Burns presented Nancy with his finest love song 'Ae Fond Kiss', set to the beautiful Gaelic air, 'Rory Dall's Port'.

This is a clear case of art transcending life, since the feeling is of a lover departing for foreign climes and service. Burns was leaving to live with his unrecognised wife, who was again pregnant and about to be thrown out of her own family home for fraternising with an immoral rhymester. Moreover, Burns had meanwhile been working off his thwarted sexual energies in a liaison with Nancy's maid, Jenny Clow.

Yet there is more to the Clarinda story than this suggests. Nancy Maclehose was a courageous and creative woman at a time when Scotswomen were discriminated against in law, and restricted in their career and cultural pathways. Born Agnes Craig, daughter of the Town Surgeon of Glasgow, Nancy and her sisters were educated and adventurous. Despite parental opposition, she was persuaded into marriage by a lawyer, James Maclehose, who turned out to be an abusive alcoholic. She left him, and in the face of prejudice against women in marital breakdowns, she fought successfully for custody of her two sons and began a new life in Edinburgh.

In the capital, the opportunities for women to participate in culture had begun to widen. Attendance at debates, assemblies or dances, concerts and theatre performances were all approved. Women discussed literature and kept journals reflecting on their reading. Nancy Maclehose aspired to start her own literary salon, and became friendly with the blind poet Thomas Blacklock, as well as Burns.

However, women participated in these activities in a private capacity, and the public climate remained censorious. When, for example, during Burns' stay in Edinburgh a male actor, James Fennell, frequented the drawing rooms of respectable ladies, this was regarded as a transgression breaching an inseparable divide between the public stage and respectable society. The theatre manager was threatened with a boycott if Fennell was not dismissed. How could the wives and daughters of Edinburgh's lairds and lawyers be exposed to professional practitioners of such dubious morality? The same question was not, of course, posed about the relationship between some of those same lairds and lawyers with the city's prostitutes.

It was therefore essential for Nancy Maclehose to avoid any public comment, far less scandal, which could threaten the custody of her children and the discreet financial support of her respectable Craig relatives. A physical relationship with the married poet was out of the question. It is unlikely that Robert Burns treated Nancy as an equal outside the correspondence of Sylvander with Clarinda. He wanted poetry and sex on his terms. Nancy's maid Jenny Clow gave birth to Burns' son, and later died in poverty in the Cowgate. She denied the poet any access to the child, who was adopted and made a success of his life.

Later too, Nancy travelled to Jamaica to attempt a reconciliation with her husband James. But she found him living with a freed slave, as was customary among the Scottish community there, and more alcohol dependent than ever. Returning to Edinburgh, she lived to a ripe old age in Calton Hill, treasuring her memories of the now-famous Robert Burns, while discreetly selling some of his letters.

Like feminism, the slavery question continued to divide Scotland into the 19th century. Some Enlightenment philosophers, such as Francis Hutcheson, who inspired both Hume and Adam Smith, taught that slavery was unequivocally wrong in all circumstances. Smith wrote that Black slaves had more magnanimity of soul than their sordid masters and that, moreover, slavery was economically inefficient in the long run.

David Hume was more ambivalent, speculating that Black people might constitute an inferior form of humanity, alleging that 'there was never a civilised nation of any complexion but white'. So much for Enlightenment history! Lord Kames, a legal luminary and speculative thinker, argued that Black people formed a different species, while acknowledging, perhaps for form's sake, that religion taught there was only one human species, created by God.

The Aberdeen philosopher James Beattie, who opposed Hume on many issues, insisted that Christianity trumped commerce. The onus, he argued, was on those who disagreed to prove 'that the produce of America and the West Indies, such as Peruvian bark, Rum and Sugar, are of more importance than justice and mercy'. In Beattie, the cause of abolition had an eloquent spokesperson, but there was a long struggle ahead to apply many of the Scottish Enlightenment's better principles in practice. In many global respects, we are still struggling.

EIGHT

The 19th Century: A Sense of Change

Wizard of the North

WALTER SCOTT, AUTHORIALLY titled Sir Walter Scott, was born in Edinburgh, the son of a lawyer who was related to the landowning Scott clan of the Borders. Due to early ill health and a club foot, some of Walter's childhood was spent with relatives at Smailholm Tower. There he began a lifelong love affair with the history, lore and songs of the Scottish Borders. In his years of success he established himself as the Laird of Abbotsford, building a heritage mansion, personal museum and home on what had formerly been known as Clarty Hole Farm by the Tweed.

Experiencing the Borders as a different kind of society from urban Edinburgh, Scott became interested in the Scottish Enlightenment ideas about stages in historical development. Scotland itself offered compelling contrasts between traditional hunter-gatherer and pastoral cultures, as in the Highlands and Border Uplands, and the agrarian and mercantile society of the Lowlands. Scott was both a hard-headed historian and immersed in traditional cultural sources.

This sets up an interesting comparison with Scott's fellow Borderer and writer, James Hogg. As a hill farm worker from childhood and later a shepherd, Hogg had minimal schooling compared to Scott's attendance at Edinburgh's High School and then University. Yet Hogg and his family were part of a rich oral culture. His mother, Margaret Laidlaw, was a noted ballad singer, and her father, Will Laidlaw, was celebrated like Robert

Kirk for his dealings with the fairy folk.

Self-educated through his own reading and his absorption of oral tradition, James Hogg became an artist in poetry and prose, but his perspective remained that of working people. This led to tensions in his relationship with Scott, who had become a prominent lawyer and Sheriff of Selkirk as well as an aspirant landowner and establishment Tory. At the same, time there are creative interactions between their books.

Walter Scott began his literary career as a translator from German and a collector of oral tradition. His *Minstrelsy of the Scottish Border*, first published in 1802 and repeatedly expanded, continues as the defining collection of Borders folksong. This led Scott into writing his own narrative verse on historical themes. Poems such as *Lay of the Last Minstrel* and *Lady of the Lake* hit a Romantic sweet spot and were enormously successful. This tempted Scott into commercial printing and publishing deals which were to have disastrous consequences for his own finances.

An early challenge came to Scott's success when his poem *Marmion*, about the Battle of Flodden, had poor sales. One day, rooting about in his attic for some fishing tackle, he stumbled on the opening of a historical novel which he had begun three years earlier and then abandoned. Scott decided to pick up where he had left off, and in three months produced *Waverley: or, 'Tis Sixty Years Since*, which was then published anonymously to immense acclaim.

Scott later admitted that it was Lord Byron's success as a poet that had knocked him off the top spot – 'Byron beat me.' Byron had in fact satirised Scott's poetry in his scathing 'English Bards and Scotch Reviewers', which bids 'a long good night to Marmion'.

These Lays of Minstrels may they be the last!
On half-strung harps whine mournful to the blast.
And thinkst thou, Scott, by vain conceit perchance
On public taste to foist thy stale romance?

Byron was the better poet, but he regretted his squib and greatly admired Scott, dying in Greece with *Quentin Durward* by his bedside.

Scott's novel writing breakthrough was remarkable for its decisive speed. Through a blend of spontaneity and design, he defined a specific moment – 60 years since – in which Jacobitism had ceased to be a political threat and become a cultural attraction. In the process, Scott devised a new form of historical novel. His work does not flow directly from earlier Scottish fiction which he admired, such as the work of Tobias Smollett or Henry Mackenzie's proto-Romantic *The Man of Feeling*. Instead, Scott fed directly off the Enlightenment historians and social philosophers, and his parallel collecting of folklore. What he then developed as a genre was to spread across the world, because of its ability to present characters in the flux of historical change.

Yet as laird and lawyer, Scott published this new fiction, as opposed to poetry, anonymously. Eventually, he stamped all his literary labours as the work of Sir Walter Scott. This respectability is still embraced and he is always called Sir Walter!

For all its influence, *Waverley* is quite a strange read. The hero, Edward Waverley, is a wimp, whereas the almost heroine, Flora McIvor, is talented and determined. Edward falls into events rather than directing them, and in the end he abandons Flora, the novel's main love interest, in favour of safe domesticity with the demure Rose Bradwardine. This has been defended on the basis that Edward is a cipher which allows us to read ourselves into the novel. How would we react and behave? The hero is swept along by events which keep us reading. The Jacobites, including Bonnie Prince Charlie, are certainly more interesting collectively than Waverley.

To understand *Waverley* and many of the historical novels that follow, we need to acknowledge the underlying 'master narrative', which Scott makes explicit in his *Tales of a Grandfather*. Conceived as a way of explaining Scotland to a grandson living in London, *Tales* burgeoned into a vivid read for all age groups, and created a pervasive popular version of Scotland's history. Not since Abbot Bower had anyone attempted to so comprehensively narrate the nation.

Scott upturned earlier chroniclers by arguing that the destiny of Scotland was to become part of a united Britain, ending centuries of war and division. The Union of Scotland and England in 1707, he argues, showed the hand of divine providence. Scottish history had ended in favour of a shared imperial mission. So why write about it? Because Scott the artist is also emotionally engaged with the epic or tragic drama of Scotland's nationhood, culminating in the failed Jacobite rising.

In *Tales of a Grandfather*, Scott presents the full heroic saga of Wallace and Bruce 'according to the old traditions of Scotland', which gives him free rein to slip the constraints of formal history. Many later conceptions derive from Scott, ranging from vivid, small-scale details such as Bruce's previously unmentioned encounter with a spider, to a sympathetic account of Mary Queen of Scots. She is depicted as a brave bearer of civilised values in the face of a barbarous aristocracy. We see Rizzio's murder at

Holyrood as Scott saw it, right down to the splashes of blood in the Queen's private chambers. Mary's death, based on eyewitness testimony, provides Scott with an extended emotional climax.

> When the Queen was seated in the fatal chair, she heard the death warrant read by Beale, the clerk to the Privy Council, with an appearance of indifference; nor did she seem more attentive to the devotional exercises of the Dean of Peterborough, in which, as a Catholic, she could not conscientiously join. She implored the mercy of Heaven, after the form prescribed by her own Church. She then prepared herself for execution, taking off such parts of her dress as might interfere with the deadly blow. The executioners offered their assistance, but she modestly refused it, saying, she had neither been accustomed to undress before so many spectators, nor to be served by such grooms of the chamber. She quietly chid her maids, who were unable to withhold their cries of lamentation, and reminded them that she had engaged for their silence. Last of all, Mary laid her head on the block, and the executioner severed it from her body with two strokes of his axe. The headsman held it up in his hand, and the Dean of Peterborough cried out, 'So perish all Queen Elizabeth's enemies!' No voice, save that of the Earl of Kent, could answer Amen: the rest were choked with sobs and tears.

But overall, Scott is divided against himself on the subject of Mary. He says that she may have been implicated in Darnley's murder, so contributing to her overthrow. Yet she conducts herself as a true Queen and Scott's sympathies are enlisted in her cause.

According to the master plan, James VI should accede to the English throne. But it is Elizabeth who colludes in Mary's death and then hypocritically denies her involvement. Like a skilful oral storyteller, Scott takes us with him in these twist and turns.

To position Scott's major novels within his master narrative is to reveal the echoes and contradictions which still make Scott a good read. The key is to push on at pace as if you were on a stage coach journey, or stuck at an airport needing imaginative diversion. Dabbling with a few pages at a time does not work, since Scott may have written faster than you are reading!

Old Mortality is Walter Scott's take on the wars of religion in Scotland's troubled 17th century. It is judged alongside *The Heart of Midlothian* as the author's best by both his son-in-law and biographer, John Gibson Lockhart, and by fellow Borderer and novelist, John Buchan. Scott's characters embody the conflict between Presbyterian Covenanters and the Royalists, while he evokes the struggle with concision, pace and dramatic intensity. The result is historically convincing and authentically grim, though there is comic relief in the shape of ordinary people caught up in a high-level war not of their making. Tragedy rubs shoulders with comedy, and religious ecstasy and madness with down-to-earth humour.

In one fine scene, Mause Headrig, torn between piety and maternal love, tries to prevent her son taking an oath of loyalty to the Royalist government.

> 'O hinny, hinny!' said she to Cuddie, hanging upon his neck, 'glad and proud and sorry and humbled am I, a' in ane and the same instant, to see my bairn ganging to testify for the truth gloriously with his mouth in council, as he did with his weapon in the field.'

'Whisht, whisht, mither!' cried Cuddie impatiently. 'Odds, ye daft wife, is this a time to speak o' thae things? I tell ye I'll testify naething either ae gate or anither. I hae spoken to Mr Poundtext, and I'll tak the Declaration, or whate'er they ca' it, and we're a' to win free off if we do that – he's gotten life for himsell and a' his folk, and that's a minister for my siller; I like nane o' your sermons that end in a psalm at the Grassmarket.'

'O, Cuddie, man, laith wad I be they suld hurt ye,' said old Mause, divided grievously between the safety of her son's soul and that of his body, 'but mind, my bonny bairn, ye hae battled for the faith, and dinna let the dread o' losing creature comforts withdraw ye frae the gude fight.'

'Hout, tout, mither,' replied Cuddie, 'I hae fought e'en ower muckle already, and, to speak plain, I'm wearied o' the trade. I hae swaggered wi' a' thae arms, and muskets and pistols, hufi-coats and bandoliers lang enough, and I like the plough-paidle a hantle better […].'

'But, my dear Cuddie,' continued the persevering Mause, 'your bridal garment! Oh, hinny, dinna sully the marriage garment.'

'Awa, awa, mither,' replied Cuddie, 'dinna ye see the folk waiting for me – Never fear me – I ken how to turn this far better than ye do – for ye're bleezing awa about marriage, and the job is how we are to win by hanging.'

Scots language is used here in different registers to express religious ideas and everyday common sense. Scott also deploys a high English style in the speech of Claverhouse, Viscount Dundee.

'But in truth, Mr Morton, why should we care so much for death, fight upon us or around us whenever it may? Men die daily – not a bell tolls the hour but it is the death-note of someone or other; and why hesitate to shorten the span of others, or take over-anxious care to prolong our own? [...] When I think of death, Mr Morton, as a thing worth thinking of, it is in the hope of pressing one day some well-fought and hard-won field of battle, and dying with the shout of victory in my ear – that would be worth dying for, and more, it would be worth having lived for!

Claverhouse in *Old Mortality* is a mix of 'Bluidy Clavers' and 'Bonnie Dundee'. But overall Scott favours 'reason' and government control against the Covenanters' determined resistance in the cause of religious liberty. At the same time, he acknowledges the emotional power of the cause, not least in the figure of Old Mortality, who devotes his life to repairing Covenanter graves and monuments across Scotland.

The Covenanters are also a touchstone of division between Walter Scott and James Hogg whose *The Brownie of Bodsbeck* is a riposte to *Old Mortality*. Hogg sympathizes with local resistance to an imposed regime, and this is the cause of a rare quarrel between the two writers. Hogg gives a vivid account of this conversation on one of his visits to Scott's house in Castle Street.

There was once more, and only once, that I found Sir Walter in the same querulous humour with me. It was the day after the publication of my Brownie of Bodsbeck. I called on him after his return from the Parliament house, on pretence of asking his advice about some very important affair, but in fact, to hear his sentiments of my new work. His shaggy eyebrows were hanging very low down, a bad prelude, which I knew too well.

'I have read through your new work, Mr. Hogg,' said he, 'and must tell you downright and plainly, as I always do, that I like it very ill – very ill indeed.'

'What for, Mr. Scott?'

'Because it is a false and unfair picture of the times and the existing characters, altogether an exaggerated and unfair picture!'

'I dinna ken, Mr. Scott. It is the picture I have been bred up in the belief o' sin' ever I was born, and I had it frae them whom I was most bound to honour and believe. An' mair nor that, there is not one single incident in the tale – not one – which I cannot prove from history, to be literally and positively true […] An' that's a great deal mair than you can say for your tale o' Auld Mortality.

'Well, well. As to its running counter to Old Mortality, I have nothing to say. Nothing in the world. I only tell you, that with the exception of Old Nanny, the crop-eared Covenanter, who is by far the best character you ever drew in your life, I dislike the tale exceedingly, and assure you it is a distorted, a prejudiced, and untrue picture of the Royal party.'

Contested memories continued to divide Scotland, with Hogg lining up not so much against Scott, whom he warmly respected, as the Enlightenment literati such as Hume, who described the

Covenanters as 'fanatics' in his commercially successful *History of England*.

Another Scott book with which to begin is *The Heart of Midlothian*, a quintessentially Edinburgh novel. The book has two main storylines which are linked by the idea of pardons. In one strand, Jeannie Deans walks to London to secure a royal pardon for her sister Effie, after refusing to testify falsely that she knew that Effie had been pregnant. Under Scots law of the time, concealment of pregnancy was a crime that could lead to the death penalty if a baby subsequently went missing. This was Effie's situation. Jeannie manages to reach the Queen in London and secure the pardon – a benevolent outcome of the Union with England.

The Deans sisters, daughters of the upright Davie Deans, are also the link with the other pardon – the story of the Porteous Riots of 1736. The father of Effie's baby is in tow with smugglers locked up in the Heart of Midlothian, the town jail. Public sympathy is with the smugglers because of the unpopular imposition of customs dues after the Union, without, so far, any compensating economic benefits.

The smugglers are sentenced to hang, but there is a riot to try and prevent the execution. Captain Porteous of the Town Guard orders his men to fire on the crowd, killing several people. He is then tried for murder, found guilty by an Edinburgh jury and himself sentenced to hang. But the day before the execution he is pardoned from London. That night, an organised operation springs him from the jail and carries out the sentence. This was justice to some but for others a lynching. Scott's narrative of these turbulent events is taut and atmospheric.

The procession now moved forward with a slow and determined pace. It was enlightened by many blazing links and torches; for the actors of this work were so far from affecting any secrecy on the occasion, that they seemed even to court observation. Their principal leaders kept close to the person of the prisoner, whose pallid yet stubborn features were seen distinctly by the torch-light, as his person was raised considerably above the concourse which thronged around him. Those who bore swords, muskets, and battle-axes, marched on each side, as if forming a regular guard to the procession. The windows, as they went along, were filled with the inhabitants, whose slumbers had been broken by this unusual disturbance. Some of the spectators muttered accents of encouragement; but in general they were so much appalled by a sight so strange and audacious, that they looked on with a sort of stupified astonishment. No one offered, by act or word, the slightest interruption [...] As they descended the Bow towards the fatal spot where they designed to complete their purpose, it was suggested that there should be a rope kept in readiness. For this purpose the booth of a man who dealt in cordage was forced open, a coil of rope fit for their purpose was selected to serve as a halter, and the dealer next morning found that a guinea had been left on his counter in exchange; so anxious were the perpetrators of this daring action to show that they meditated not the slightest wrong or infraction of law, excepting so far as Porteous was himself concerned.

The influence of this narrative craft can be seen in Thomas Carlyle's *History of the French Revolution*, and in Charles Dickens'

Oliver Twist when Nancy's murderer is pursued over the rooftops.

The Heart of Midlothian also contains some of Scott's strongest characterisations including Madge Wildfire, who roams Arthur's Seat in search of her own lost child, and the doughty Davie Deans. They are backed by a chorus of Edinburgh worthies, who comment on the action.

> 'And as for the lords of state,' said Miss Dalmahoy, 'ye suld mind the riding o' the parliament, Mr Saddletree, in the guid auld time before the Union, – a year's rent o' mony a gude estate gaed for horse-graith and harnessing, forby broidered robes and foot-mantles, that wad hae stude by their lane wi' gold brocade, and that were muckle in my ain line.'
>
> 'Ay, and then the lusty banqueting, with sweetmeats and comfits wet and dry, and dried fruits of divers sorts,' said Pludamas. 'But Scotland was Scotland in these days.'
>
> 'I'll tell you what it is, neighbours,' said Mrs Howden, 'I'll ne'er believe Scotland is Scotland ony mair, if our kindly Scots sit doun wi' the affront they gien us this day.'

This range of dramatic voices led to Scott being dubbed 'Scotland's Shakespeare', and stage adaptations of Scott's novels were soon to solve the national drama question. Beginning at the Theatre Royal in Edinburgh, where Burns' aspirations had been thwarted, Scott's popular storylines and actable characters, such as Baillie Nicol Jarvie in *Rob Roy*, soon filled theatres across Scotland.

A less resolved aspect of *The Heart of Midlothian* is Jeannie's motivation. The refusal to tell a lie, even to save her sister's life, is grounded in religious conscience. Scott is a psychological realist and religious motivations are not in his normal range. He covers Jeannie's purpose structurally because her quest for a pardon is successful, but is more comfortable with externalising religious behaviour. This again contrasts with James Hogg, whose *The Private Memoirs and Confessions of a Justified Sinner*, set in the Borders and in Edinburgh, probes religious motivation. His profound understanding of the Calvinist mentality and how it can go horribly wrong is well ahead of Scott. Hogg, for whom traditional culture points a middle way, also warns against Enlightenment disdain for religion.

Walter Scott's imagination reached out towards gothic fantasy, as the contents of Abbotsford show, but he was private and moderate in religion, and stoical in the face of life's hard knocks. This was just as well, since the high peak of his fortunes was followed by dire reverse as he was sucked into a financial crash by guarantees he had provided to the publisher Archibald Constable. Scott was allowed to live on at Abbotsford by bankruptcy trustees, but laboured for the rest of his life to pay off the enormous debts.

To this toughest stretch belongs another classic of life writing, Scott's *Journal*. Not intended for publication, the terse entries reveal Scott accounting for every penny to make ends meet, losing any joy in literary creation, working on when miserably ill and confessing his fury at the indifference of the British government towards Scotland's national traditions. And all this while still performing his public legal duties, and enduring uncongenial lodging in Edinburgh. Yet along the way there are observations which catch your breath.

Burke the Murderer hanged this morning. The mob which
was immense demanded Knox (the Anatomist) and Hare
but though greedy for more victims received with shouts the
solitary wretch who found his way to the gallows out of five
or six who seem not less guilty than He. But the story begins
to be stale in so much that I believe a doggerel ballad upon
it would be popular how brutal soever the wit. This is the
progress of human passions. We ejaculate exclaim hold up to
heaven our hand like the rustic Phidele – next morning the
mood changes and we dance a jig to the tune which moved us
to tears.

The Journal records a struggle that Scott cannot ultimately win,
but he did clear the debt, at enormous personal cost, and, after a
final European journey, made it home to Abbotsford in 1832 to die.

The Sage of Ecclefechan

Thomas Carlyle is a supreme example of a humble 'lad o pairts'
excelling through learning. Hailing from the village of Ecclefechan
in Dumfriesshire, his education was supported by devoted parents
at Annan Academy and then Edinburgh University. There Carlyle
soaked up every aspect of Scottish Enlightenment thinking, and
much European literature besides. Though excelling in mathematics
and science, he was more attracted to philosophy and languages.

After graduation, he began training to be a Presbyterian minister but soon dropped out and stayed on in Edinburgh, battling
to earn a living from writing articles for periodicals and ency-

clopedias. With both *The Edinburgh Review* and *Blackwood's Magazine* well-established, Edinburgh was a thriving centre for this form of publishing. Carlyle also branched into translation with a focus on German literature.

In 1827 Thomas Carlyle's essay 'Signs of the Times' was published in *The Edinburgh Review*. This proved to be a game-changer in British social thought, and marks the moment Carlyle emerged as an original thinker and defining 'prophet' of the later Victorian era. In 'Signs of the Times' he accuses society of being enslaved to a mechanistic way of thinking in economic, social and intellectual life. Materialistic 'causes and effects' had displaced human character as the moving force in human affairs. Relationships of love and trust had been subordinated, not just in society but in people's personal lives as well.

The essay is eloquent in a hard-hitting and persuasive style. A new voice had emerged; it was to energise many other key 19th-century figures including Charles Dickens, John Ruskin, Ralph Waldo Emerson and William Morris. By the end of his long career, Carlyle had become limited by his prophetic stance, but in these earlier years in Edinburgh, and then in London, he wove different voices and personas into his rhetorical art.

In 1832–3 Thomas Carlyle's novel *Sartor Resartus* was serialised in *Fraser's Magazine*. The main character is Dionysius Teufelsdröckh, or 'Zeus born devil's dung foot', a kind of philosophic Tristram Shandy. He is, in turn, writing a book *Clothes, Their Origin and Influence*. Like Abbot Sampson in Carlyle's subsequent *Past and Present*, Teufelsdröckh is a humorous, fantastic channel for Carlylean perceptions and linguistic bravura.

Sartor Resartus also expresses Carlyle's 'Everlasting Yea', an affirmation of faith as experienced by the author on Leith Walk when going for a daily swim in the Forth. This captures another culture changing moment, in which Carlyle defines his new religious sensibility, strongly influenced by German idealism. This sensibility, Carlyle claims, transcends creeds and denominations. Through the 'Everlasting Yea', Carlyle harnessed an international transformation while loosening the previously immovable bond between traditional Presbyterianism and Scottish culture.

Modern Scotland is hugely influenced by Thomas Carlyle without generally knowing anything about him. Here is a flavour of *Sartor Resartus* in which a vison of Yea displaces the 'Everlasting No'.

> May we not say, however, that the hour of Spiritual Enfranchisement is even this: When your Ideal World, wherein the whole man has been dimly struggling and inexpressibly languishing to work, becomes revealed, and thrown open; and you discover, with amazement enough, like the Lothario in Wilhelm Meister, that your 'America is here or nowhere'? The Situation that has not its Duty, its Ideal, was never yet occupied by man. Yes here or nowhere is thy Ideal: work it out therefrom; and working, believe, live, be free. Fool! the Ideal is in thyself, the impediment too is in thyself [...] the thing thou seekest is already with thee [...] couldst thou only see!
>
> But it is with man's Soul as it was with Nature: the beginning of Creation is Light. Till the eye have vision, the whole members are in bonds. Divine moment, when over the tempest-tost Soul, as once over the wild-weltering Chaos, it is spoken: Let there be Light! [...] The mad primeval Dis-

cord is hushed; the rudely-jumbled conflicting elements bind themselves into separate Firmaments: deep silent rock-foundations are built beneath; and the skyey vault with its everlasting Luminaries above: instead of a dark wasteful Chaos, we have a blooming, fertile, heaven-encompassed World.

I too could now say to myself: Be no longer a Chaos, but a World, or even Worldkin. Produce! Produce! Were it but the pitifullest infinitesimal fraction of a Product, produce it, in God's name! 'Tis the utmost thou hast in thee: out with it, then. Up, up! Whatsoever thy hand findeth to do, do it with thy whole might. Work while it is called Today; for the Night cometh, wherein no man can work.

This is Carlyle's 'natural supernaturalism' which is directly expressed in the world's flow. It is also his holy Gospel of work, without which order cannot be created out of the chaos and violence in which the 19th century felt itself embroiled.

Carlyle went on to demonstrate this in his 1837 *History of the French Revolution*, which sealed his reputation as a defining writer of the age. Working at red-hot pace, Carlyle captures a vivid sense of history in the making. His text exists in the past present, reconstructing events dramatically as if in a novel, while simultaneously expanding his core themes of social decay, destruction and reform. Though writing at speed, Carlyle often destroyed his drafts and furiously rewrote. This is notoriously true of the first whole part of *History of the French Revolution*, which the author had lent to John Stuart Mill for comment. A maid, seeing the dog-eared and blotted pages, used them to light a bedroom fire. Such was Carlyle's creative workshop.

Though London became Thomas Carlyle's main base, he did not lose touch with Scotland. In 1865 he was elected Rector of Edinburgh University, and in the same decade he produced the successful blueprint for a Scottish National Portrait Gallery, similar to the National Portrait Gallery in London which he had also helped to establish. The Portrait Gallery remains a much-loved Edinburgh institution and a reminder of Carlyle's belief that human psychology is the defining force in history. In the face of catastrophic human-induced climate change, we can see the force of that view and its limitations.

For most of his working life, Carlyle was in close partnership with his ever-perceptive wife, Jane Welsh Carlyle, who was born in Haddington and had lived in George Square in Edinburgh. Jane outdid Thomas as an artist of the letter, and their joint voluminous correspondence is still being edited and printed. After her death in 1866, Carlyle wrote *Reminiscences*, a painfully sincere autobiography which is structured around memories of the most important people in his life. The revelation of Carlyle's failures as a husband and companion to Jane had a negative impact on his Victorian reputation, but now looks courageously open-eyed.

Reminiscences is another fine example of Scottish literature's achievements in life writing. Carlyle was also a biographer, and a biographical essayist, writing insightfully on James Boswell, Robert Burns and Walter Scott.

Margaret Oliphant

In the early 19th century, Scott and Hogg were not the only fresh talents. John Galt provided a distinctive and often satiric voice, while a number of women novelists successfully made their mark. These included Mary Brunton, Susan Ferrier, Elizabeth Hamilton and Christian Johnston. At the same time, Joanna Baillie won recognition for her poems and plays. But this group were all to be overtaken by the enormous productivity of Margaret Oliphant as a professional woman of letters. Mrs Oliphant, as she chose to be known, wrote 90 novels, plus biography and literature of place, as well as hundreds of periodical essays and reviews, establishing herself as the in-house essayist and reviewer for *Blackwood's Magazine.*

It is hard to digest or assess the Oliphant output, but she is a significant innovator in Scottish and English literature, because her main subject is the lives of women, which she explores through her own complex challenges as a mother, wife, widow, carer and breadwinner. Oliphant lost her husband early to ill-health and, in the course of time, all of her three children. She also cared for a mentally ill brother and his three children.

Inevitably these responsibilities and the necessity to earn hampered Oliphant's ability to write in the way she wanted. Her output is often described as 'uneven', but Margaret Oliphant herself upheld high critical standards, and would want her work judged without excuses. Autobiographical questioning is integral to her writing and one of its main strengths. In a sense, she is always writing her own life with its multiple ups and downs. That is the route through which she creates diverse characters and sheds new light on the experiences of women in general.

At the end of her long and full life, Oliphant wrote *The Story of My Days* which shirks none of the heart-breaking challenges and the despairs she had faced. The autobiography was mauled on first publication by well-meaning relatives, but has been restored by modern scholarship to its rightful place as an exemplar of the genre. Mrs Oliphant always knew what she was doing, while acknowledging that not everything she had undertaken in life or art was successful.

Margaret Wilson was born in Wallyford, near Edinburgh, and brought up in Glasgow and Liverpool. Her short married life was spent with her artist husband and cousin, Frank Oliphant, in London and Italy. She settled as a widow in Windsor to raise her children and other dependents. Her most immediately successful works were *The Chronicles of Carlingford* which compare with Trollope's *The Barchester Chronicles* while focussing on non-conformist English society.

But Margaret Oliphant continued to be distinctively Scottish in outlook and language. She was often north of the Border and managed most of her literary affairs in tandem with Blackwood publishers in Edinburgh. There is a strong argument that much of her finest writing is set in Scotland because of her connection with its landscape, social life, psychology and religion. She was also a close student of Scottish literature, and produces her own commentary on Walter Scott's national narrative from the perspective of women through different historic periods.

Early in her career, Mrs Oliphant produced *Katie Stewart: A True Story*. Originating in her mother's family traditions, the novel is set in the East Neuk of Fife at the time of the 1745 Jacobite

Rising. It seems like a domestic novel about the relationship between two households – the Erskine lairds of Kellie Castle and the Stewart family at the local mill, which includes their youngest daughter, Kate. She becomes a favourite at the castle and goes to live there, experiencing some of the Erskine's Jacobite connections. But this is limited to impacts on family life.

Katie Stewart exhibits Oliphant's hallmark strengths in its depiction of contrasting female characters and its fluent command of spoken Scots. But the novel moves powerfully beyond the domestic in its account of press-gangs raiding the East Neuk ports, ambushing incoming boats and cruelly tearing families apart in the name of king and country.

> Eagerly running along by the edge of the rocks, at a pace which, on another Sabbath, she would have thought a desecration of the day, clinging to Willie Morison's arm, and with an anxious heart, feeling her presence a kind of protection to him, Katie Stewart hastens to the Billowness. The grey pier of Anster is lined with anxious faces, and here and there a levelled telescope [...] The tide is out, and venturous lads are stealing along the sharp low ranges of rock, slipping now and then with incautious steps into the little clear pools of sea-water which surround them; for their eyes are not on their own uncertain footing, but fixed, like the rest, on that visible danger up the Firth, in which all feel themselves concerned.
>
> Already there are spectators, and another telescope on the Billowness, and the whole range of 'the braes' between Anstruther and Pittenweem is dotted with anxious lookers-on; and the

far-away pier of Pittenweem, too, is dark with its little crowd.

What is the cause? Not far from the shore, just where that headland, which hides from you the deep indentation of Largo Bay, juts out upon the Firth, lies a little vessel, looking like a diminutive Arabian horse, or one of the aristocratic young slight lads who are its officers, with high blood, training, and courage, in every tight line of its cordage, and taper stretch of its masts. Before it, arrested in its way, lies a helpless merchant brig, softly swaying on the bright mid-waters of the Firth, with the cutter's boat rapidly approaching its side.

Another moment and it is boarded; a very short interval of silence, and again the officer – you can distinguish him with that telescope by his cocked-hat, and the flash which the scabbard of his sword throws on the water as he descends the vessel's side – has re-entered the cutter's boat. Heavily the boat moves through the water now, crowded with pressed men – poor writhing hearts, whose hopes of home-coming and peace have been blighted in a moment.

In *Magdalen Herbert*, a later historical novel, Mrs Oliphant continues her atmospheric evocation of land and sea, focussing again on east coast settings – St Andrews and the Tay, the Lammermuirs and the Forth, and Berwick at Tweedmouth. This novel tackles the Scottish Reformation head on and succeeds in evoking the early Protestant grassroots as forerunners of the Covenanting spirit. Despite a range of strong female characters and consummate Scots dialogue, *Magdalen Herbert* is weakened by Oliphant's decision to adopt an imitative period style, which clogs her normal fluency. Also the personal story is overextended in order to fit the long curve of public events. Despite this, the novel contains the most convincing portrait of John Knox as an individual in Scottish literature.

Late in her long career, Margaret Oliphant wrote *Kirsteen*, which is generally recognised as her finest Scottish novel. The story begins in 1814, the year that *Waverley* was published, which is not accidental given that the book's full title echoes Scott – *Kirsteen: The Story of a Scotch Family Seventy Years Ago*. Oliphant's version is still post-Jacobite in that she traces the long-term decline of Highland culture and the psychological bleakness that results. Yet against this Oliphant pits her hero, a young modern woman who achieves independent success, breaking free from her struggling upper-class family and in particular her violent father. Kirsteen establishes herself as a successful businesswoman in London, working in textiles and fashion, and then moves to Edinburgh's New Town as a woman of independent means. Perhaps that is where Margaret Oliphant herself would like to have finally settled, had circumstances allowed.

Kirsteen was serialised in *Macmillan's Magazine*, in which some of Thomas Hardy's novels first appeared, and it is striking to see Mrs Oliphant moving from being a mid-Victorian author into the late 19th century. Her admirers were the emergent stars, such as Robert Louis Stevenson and JM Barrie. Even Henry James, when pressed, had to admit the freshness and vigour of *Kirsteen*. But generally he was irritated by Oliphant and depicted her unpleasantly as the vulgar and talentless Mrs Stormer in his short story 'Greville Fane'. This seems to have been mansplaining in response to Oliphant's shrewd critical writing. Trollope also traduced Mrs Oliphant as Lady Carbury in his novel *The*

Way We Live Now, and Hardy called her 'a perfect priestess indeed – of the Commonplace'. In response, Oliphant remained unimpressed by Henry James' women characters, and was happy to be described as connecting with a wide readership!

Another aspect of Margaret Oliphant that makes her an illuminating presence in 19th-century fiction is her exploration of religious belief. She openly professed Christianity as core to her sense of existence, but pushed questioning boundaries in her novels and her supernatural stories, which she collected as *Tales of the Seen and Unseen*. These finely crafted stories, in some cases novellas, move beyond speculation to encompass experiences that unexpectedly percolate into everyday life and challenge normal boundaries.

Short fictions such as 'The Secret Chamber', 'The Portrait' and 'The Library Window', and her novella 'The Beleaguered City', demonstrate a high level of literary craft. The prose seems to operate on a naturalistic level, while hovering on the edge of something beyond realistic experience, yet somehow inevitable.

> Lord Gowrie was very grave and very pale. He was standing with his hand on his son's shoulder to wake him; his dress was unchanged from the moment they had parted, and the sight of this costume was very bewildering to the young man as he started up in his bed. But next moment he seemed to know exactly how it was, and, more than that, to have known it all his life. Explanation seemed unnecessary.

Untrammelled and undistracted, Margaret Oliphant stands in the front rank of 19th century writers on her own terms.

Tusitala

Robert Louis Stevenson is the great stylist of 19th-century Scottish literature, and a gateway towards the modern. He writes with economy, suppleness and grace. Every novel, story, poem and even letter feels like a new creation in real time.

Like Scott and Oliphant, Stevenson uses Scots dialogue but English in prose narrative, yet his English evinces a muscular underlay of Scots where Walter Scott is more formally extended. You sense in Stevenson the language of the makars, the prose of John Knox, the King James Bible and the intellectual clarity of the Enlightenment, all blended with fresh psychological insight and imaginative purpose.

Stevenson's talent seems to spring into life fully grown with *Treasure Island* in 1883. The book has come to define novels of adventure as a genre, but the narrative approach taps into centuries of Scots storytelling.

I remember him as if it were yesterday, as he came plodding to the inn door, his sea-chest following behind him in a hand-barrow; a tall, strong, heavy, nut-brown man; his tarry pigtail falling over the shoulders of his soiled blue coat; his hands ragged and scarred, with black, broken nails; and the sabre-cut along one cheek, a dirty, livid white. I remember him looking round the cove and whistling to himself as he did so, and then breaking out in that old sea-song that he sang so often afterwards:
  'Fifteen men on the dead man's chest –
  Yo-ho-ho, and a bottle of rum!'

The progression is artful, as Blind Pew's sinister delivery of the 'black spot' to this sea-dog is followed by the arrival of the other pirates in search of the map from which the tale unfolds.

Treasure Island has dark undercurrents. None of the protagonists witnessed by Jim Hawkins, the young narrator, evidence enlightened motives or unsullied behaviour. The greatest villain of the piece, Long John Silver, is a plausible deceiver, a false narrator and a callous killer. But he is the ship's cook, not the pirate archetype beloved of film and television adaptations. It is a subtle portrayal of evil – ever ready to smooth over difficulties while pulling the shadowy strings. Even in extremity, Silver is ready with another deceit and in the end he escapes justice, making off with a share of the loot. *Treasure Island* is an adventure story which treats children as adults, while giving adult readers permission to enjoy the action as well as the motivations.

Kidnapped, The Master of Ballantrae and *Catriona* comprise Stevenson's extended take on the Jacobites. Though all three include journeys of adventure, the focus is on the psycho-cultural clash between Highland and Lowland. This is skilfully embodied in *Kidnapped*'s relationship between David Balfour and the Jacobite officer, Alan Breck Stewart. Storytelling and characterisation combine in a subtle harmony that expresses conflict. From the moment that David's miserly Uncle Ebenezer tries to kill him, the narrative never slackens till we find ourselves back outside the half-ruined tower where David is finally able, with Alan's help, to claim his inheritance.

Catriona, which was written in Samoa, is a more political tale of intrigue. Having witnessed imperial oppression in the South Seas at first hand, Stevenson revisits the repression of Highland culture and society after the Jacobite Rising of 1745–6. In particular he focuses on the confiscation of estates and the violent reaction, including the unjust trial and execution of James Stewart of Appin for the murder of Colin Campbell. In Stevenson's version, the more likely suspect is Alan Breck Stewart. These events are treated with historical seriousness, which outweighs the love interest between the heroes Catriona and David Balfour.

The Master of Ballantrae is a psychological thriller embodied in the relationship between two brothers and culminating in a journey into the far north of America. On the toss of a coin, one brother – the Master – 'goes out' with Bonnie Prince Charlie while the other, dutiful Henry, is kept at home to demonstrate loyalty to the establishment. This stark duality becomes more complex through our dependence on the estate steward Mackellar, who proves to be an unreliable narrator. The Master may sometimes behave like a devil incarnate, but the supposedly upright Henry is consumed by jealousy and a potentially murderous hatred of his brother.

The unifying drive is again a compulsion to tell the tale and fold us into the drama. In this regard, Mackellar is Stevenson's proxy.

The full truth of this odd matter is what the world has long
been looking for, and public curiosity is sure to welcome.
It so befell that I was intimately mingled with the last years
and history of the house; and there does not live one man so
able as myself to make these matters plain, or so desirous to
narrate them faithfully. I knew the Master; on many secret
steps of his career I have an authentic memoir in my hand; I
sailed with him on his last voyage almost alone; I made one
upon that winter's journey of which so many tales have gone

abroad; and I was there at the man's death. As for my late Lord Durrisdeer, I served him and loved him near twenty years; and thought more of him the more I knew of him. Altogether, I think it not fit that so much evidence should perish; the truth is a debt I owe my lord's memory; and I think my old years will flow more smoothly, and my white hair lie quieter on the pillow, when the debt is paid.

Before the end we are compelled to question the nature of this 'authentic memoir' and the debt that is paid. Stevenson moves closer in this novel to James Hogg.

Divided selves are even more prominent in another genre-defying Stevenson novel, *The Strange case of Dr Jekyll and Mr Hyde*. Though nominally set in London, the atmosphere of this Gothic thriller belongs to Edinburgh where two towns coexist side by side – the classically ordered New Town and the dark wynds of the Old Town, where addiction, prostitution and crime proliferated. This is the theatre of Stevenson's youth.

The narrative strategy of *Dr Jekyll and Mr Hyde* is different from previous novels. The framework is formal and restrained, only teasing at underlying problems, until gradually puzzles give way to mystery, perplexity and the inference of horror. The novel as we have it is a re-write from an earlier dream-driven fantasy which Stevenson's wife Fanny Osbourne insisted he should revise. The final outcome is good because the dream underlay of the novel is suppressed and therefore all the more unsettling. This is demonstrated by the many stage and film adaptations which try to visualise what Stevenson only suggests in indirect narratives, concluding with Henry Jekyll's account.

It is useless, and the time awfully fails me, to prolong this description; no one has ever suffered such torments, let that suffice; and yet even to these, habit brought – no, not alleviation – but a certain callousness of soul, a certain acquiescence of despair; and my punishment might have gone on for years, but for the last calamity which has now fallen, and which has finally severed me from my own face and nature. My provision of the salt, which had never been renewed since the date of the first experiment, began to run low. I sent out for a fresh supply and mixed the draught; the ebullition followed, and the first change of colour, not the second; I drank it and it was without efficiency [...]

But a week has passed, and I am now finishing this statement under the influence of the last of the old powders. This, then, is the last time, short of a miracle, that Henry Jekyll can think his own thoughts or see his own face (now how sadly altered!) in the glass. Nor must I delay too long to bring my writing to an end; for if my narrative has hitherto escaped destruction, it has been by a combination of great prudence and great good luck. Should the throes of change take me in the act of writing it, Hyde will tear it in pieces; but if some time shall have elapsed after I have laid it by, his wonderful selfishness and circum-scription to the moment will probably save it once again from the action of his ape-like spite.

When Robert Louis Stevenson came to write his last unfinished Scottish novel, *Weir of Hermiston*, he and Fanny were settled in Samoa. During his five years there, Stevenson wrote about the history and traditional culture of the South Seas. He supported the

Samoans against the competing imperialisms of Britain, Germany and the USA, and he celebrated Pacific myth and legend. For all this he was accorded the title 'Tusitala' – Storyteller. In the same period he crafted resonant tales about European drop-outs – the beach wrack of imperialism – and the degradation of tribal society. These works point forward to the 20th century and modern Scottish literature.

In *Weir of Hermiston*, however, Stevenson was consciously looking back and coming to terms with his own Scottishness. Archie Weir, the young hero, is connected through his mother's lands of Hermiston with the Borders and Covenanting times. His father, Lord Weir, is Scotland's senior judge, and that side of the novel is set in the Edinburgh of James Boswell's Journals, right down to Archie's opposition to unwarranted sentences of death casually handed down by the courts. The father and son conflict of *Weir of Hermiston* also recalls Boswell, though Weir is modelled on the 18th-century 'hanging judge' Lord Braxfield.

Young Archie's studies are shaped by Edinburgh's Enlightenment, adopting English manners and language; he reads moral philosophy and attends the University's Speculative Society. His father retains broad Scots speech and reductive sarcasm. But Archie's emotional connection is with his dead mother, which is continued through Kirstie, the housekeeper at Hermiston. It is there that tragedy is played out with the passions of a Scots ballad.

> 'Eh, lad, and that's easy sayin,' cried Kirstie, 'but it's nane sae easy doin! Man, do ye no comprehend that it's God's wull we should be blendit and glamoured, and have nae command over our ain members at a time like that? My bairn,' she

cried, still holding his hand, 'think o' the puir lass! have pity upon her, Erchie! and O, be wise for twa! Think o' the risk she rins! I have seen ye, and what's to prevent ithers! I saw ye once in the Hags, in my ain howf, and I was wae to see ye there – in pairt for the omen, for I think there's a weird on the place – and in pairt for pure nakit envy and bitterness o' hairt. It's strange ye should forgather there tae! God! but yon puir, thrawn, auld Covenanter's seen a heap o' human natur since he lookit his last on the musket barrels, if he never saw nane afore,' she added, with a kind of wonder in her eyes.

Sadly, Stevenson died of a haemorrhage aged 44 at his home in Vailima, having worked all morning at the unfinished novel. He was buried with full Samoan honours on nearby Mount Vaea, and his house is preserved as a national monument. Edinburgh has always claimed Robert Louis Stevenson as its own with plaques, statues, trails and anniversaries, but there is no grave, and the city has not shown much interest in the vital Samoan years. Yet perhaps Stevenson himself would have understood that, as he dedicated *Weir of Hermiston* to Fanny with this poem.

> I saw rain falling and the rainbow drawn
> On Lammermuir. Hearkening I heard again
> In my precipitous city beaten bells
> Winnow the keen sea wind. And here afar,
> Intent on my own race and place, I wrote.

Usually the quotation ends there, but Stevenson continued with a generous tribute, recognising Fanny, for all the struggles of their relationship, as a creative partner.

> Take thou the writing: thine it is. For who
> Burnished the sword, blew on the drowsy coal,
> Held still the target higher, chary of praise
> And prodigal of counsel – who but thou?
> So now, in the end, if this the least be good,
> If any deed be done, if any fire
> Burn in the imperfect page, the praise be thine.

The praise is just, for without Fanny Osbourne's support this son of Edinburgh could not have become a shining light for Scottish and world literature.

NINE

The 20th and 21st Centuries: City of Stage and Page

Peter Pan

SCOTLAND'S 20TH CENTURY began literature-wise with JM Barrie's *Peter Pan*, which was first staged in 1904. A child of Kirriemuir in Angus and then a schoolboy in Dumfries, Barrie studied literature at Edinburgh University. His first job was as drama critic for *The Edinburgh Evening Courant*.

James Barrie is the most misunderstood of Scotland's major writers, partly because he often disguised his intent. Descried as quaint and sentimental, Barrie's work is driven by an icy intellect and bleak pessimism. Though his early stories and novels play with stereotypes of Scottishness, Barrie found his form in drama through which he honed an impersonal art, while still filling theatres across the world.

Immersing himself in the techniques and mechanics of theatre, Barrie learned that his texts were only one part of a whole which involved music, movement and visual form. In his quest to realise an objective work of art, Barrie attended rehearsals, writing and rewriting, and anticipating the later role of theatre directors. For *Peter Pan*, he provided different endings, never finally settling on his preference. Things had ultimately to be worked out in performance with live audiences. Barrie had great respect for successful theatre makers, despite the denigration of actors which persisted in his Presbyterian cultural background. Even today the fact that Barrie was a popular playwright seems to undermine his rightful place in the literary pantheon. Yet, like George Bernard Shaw, he presented his plays in a different form for readers with extended stage directions and commentary.

Behind his popular work, JM Barrie was also a profound thinker, brooding on Darwin, Ibsen and Nietzsche. For him, theatre was a collective laboratory in which people came close to the evolutionary process driving nature and human consciousness. In *Peter Pan* Barrie created a modern myth, like Mary Shelley's *Frankenstein*, while remaining in the mainstream of popular culture.

The myth of the boy who could not grow up tapped into powerful Barrie obsessions. First there was the mysterious interplay between change (a law of life) and what might be changeless, perhaps through the magic of memory and of art. Then there was the incomprehensible change of death – 'that very big adventure' – that cannot be avoided. Or can it? Barrie's drama puts the onus of faith and choice on the audience to decide.

> Peter: Her light is growing faint, and if it goes out, that means she is dead! Her voice is so low I can scarcely tell what she is saying. She says – she says she thinks she could get well again if children believed in fairies. Do you believe in fairies? Say quick that you believe! If you believe, clap your hands![4]

This is an artfully constructed but unforgettable moment for children, and for adult proxies.

For Barrie himself, these difficult questions were rooted in childhood, especially the death of his older brother David in a skating accident. Young James was there on the day and felt guilty that, despite his best efforts, he could not be a substitute for his mother's beloved elder son. This lifelong trauma worked itself out through the boy who could not grow up and the lost boys. Tragically, this foreshadowed the disastrous loss of young lives in World War 1, which Barrie experienced directly through the children of his adopted Llewellyn Davies family.

In 1922 Barrie shared his inmost thoughts in an address to the students of the University of St Andrews after they had elected him their Rector. This was a crafted performance with character voices, the absent presence of the University's lost boys and a culminating prop in the shape of the letter sent by Scott of the Antarctic to Barrie shortly before the explorer's death. All Barrie's antitheses of change, changelessness and death are at work, but the core message is not to trust the older generation who sent young people to their deaths. Take things into your own hands, urges Barrie, or there will be another war. Published as *Courage*, this address exhibits Barrie's underlying pessimism but also his understanding that love and art can lend consolation and meaning. In this performance he reveals himself as a courageous existentialist.

JM Barrie's illustrious theatre career ended in Edinburgh in 1937 with the first performance of his last play *The Boy David*. Though well-received on the night, this more conventional tragedy, based on the biblical story of David and Johnathan, did not find a lasting place in the Barrie repertoire alongside plays such as *What Every Woman Knows*, *Mary Rose* or *Dear Brutus*. Barrie himself was too ill to attend his last play, remaining in a hotel bedroom in the city, dependent on his loyal administrator Cynthia Asquith for news of how it had gone in performance – his ultimate test. Such experiences are elusive and transitory, yet Barrie deserves to be remembered with greater understanding.

Patrick Geddes

Another important writer who flourished in the late 19th and early 20th centuries was Patrick Geddes. Beginning as a biologist and zoologist, Geddes moved into social science and what he called 'civics' – a combination of town planning, education and cultural activism.

Born in 1854, Geddes was an inheritor of Enlightenment thought as it developed in the 19th century with Thomas Carlyle in literature, D'Arcy Thompson in biology, the astronomy of Mary Somerville, the mathematical physics of Lord Kelvin and James Clerk Maxwell, and the philosophy of James Ferrier. It is a common mistake to imagine that the Scottish Enlightenment petered out in 1800.

For Geddes, like Barrie, evolution was the key concept, but Geddes is more optimistic, seeing human evolution as a dynamic process combining nature and consciousness. Co-operation is more important in Geddes' approach than competition, and the further development goes, the more conscious interactions matter – science, society, culture and the arts all play their part. It is that human dimension, fostered by education and creativity, which makes change positive. Geddes summed this up to his students in Dundee in a farewell address.

Star wonder, stone and spark-wonder, life-wonder and folk-wonder: these are the stuff of astronomy and physics, of biology and the social sciences [...] To appreciate sunset and sunrise, moon and stars, and the wonders of the wind, clouds and rain, the beauty of the woods and moon and fields – here are the beginning of the natural sciences.

We need to give everyone the outlook of the artist, who begins with the art of seeing, and then in time we shall follow him into the seeing of art, even the creating of it.

A general and educational point of view must be brought to bear on every specialism [...] We must cease to think merely in terms of separated departments and faculties and must relate these in the living mind; in the social mind as well – indeed this above all.

Geddes encapsulates this in his mottos: 'By Living We Learn' and 'By Creating We Think'.

Among Patrick Geddes' most important publications is *Cities in Evolution* (1915), but he was happiest teaching in 'a living laboratory', and his principal laboratory was Edinburgh. Here he jump-started a movement to re-purpose and restore older buildings, to pioneer modern social housing and to generate a new cultural renaissance in the city, with forms of artistic endeavour that tap collective energies like those of natural evolution. He published *The Evergreen: A Northern Season* devoted, like Allan Ramsay's *The Evergreen*, to 'sympathy, synergy and synthesis' between literature, the visual arts and music. Geddes was also a lightning rod for the Arts and Crafts Movement of 'hand, heart and soul', and for the Celtic Revival, which took a Pan-Celtic inspiration from James Macpherson's *Poems of Ossian* into contemporary arts and architecture.

All of these Geddes activities operated locally, regionally, nationally and internationally. There was also a performative dimension to the Geddes whirlwind. Long before the Edinburgh Festival was conceived, Geddes convened International Summer

Schools in the city in August, where students experienced creative synthesis in real time. He also organised masques and pageants, some of which he published as *Dramatisations of History*, though the texts alone fall short of the all-round theatre experience which he, like Barrie, advocated. The volunteer production teams must have been exhausted!

At the top of the Royal Mile, Geddes transformed a former observatory into his Outlook Tower, a three-dimensional thinking laboratory. His delight was to lead people to the top, at pace, to absorb the magnificent views of Edinburgh between sea and land. Then you could take in the internal reflection of the camera obscura, reminding participants that perception is vital to knowledge. On successive lower levels there were visual displays on Edinburgh, Scotland, the English speaking world, Europe and the planet. Geddes' new combination of planning and civics took him to India, Palestine, France and America, but Edinburgh remained the lodestar.

Tragically, it was in India that Geddes heard of the death of his oldest son, Alasdair, in World War I. He found himself unable to tell his wife, who died shortly afterwards. Yet Geddes argued that the best way of advancing 'the great cause – national, European, human – for which our sons have died is to take our share in preparing others to live farther.' Geddes died in 1932 still working non-stop from his Edinburgh home and still living out another motto – 'Think Global, Act Local'.

Patrick Geddes is remembered today in Edinburgh through the green spaces he created – urban lungs – the buildings he conserved, not least Riddle's Court, and the creation of Ramsay Gardens around Allan Ramsay's house. In a garden in The Netherbow area, there is a fine sculpture by Kenny Hunter set on a beehive plinth, and in the Scottish National Portrait Gallery there is a portrait bust by CJ Pibworth. These cast Geddes in the bearded mode of a bard or seer. If not prophetic, most of his ideas seem more relevant now than ever.

Hugh MacDiarmid

Another major writer, and one influenced by Patrick Geddes' philosophy of synthesis, was the poet Hugh MacDiarmid. He also figures as a long-maned Celtic seer in a 1962 portrait by Robert Heriot Westwater. In this portrait, and in a 1979 study by Alexander Moffat, MacDiarmid appears with a far-seeing gaze amidst mountain, sea and sky – reflecting human consciousness within the forces of natural evolution. In contrast, a reluctant James Barrie is portrayed in the Scottish National Portrait Gallery by William Nicolson between rehearsals for *Peter Pan*. He looks aslant, in an anonymous suit, more interested in the costumes he was working with. 'I have long ceased to be on speaking terms with my face,' he commented, 'so why have it painted?'

MacDiarmid was taken up with the evolution of consciousness in political as well as cultural and scientific terms. With Geddes he shared a cosmic sense in which planet earth and its natural forms connected humanity with the Universe, though MacDiarmid's concept of Scotland's place in that wider field was sharp and distinctive.

> The rose of all the world is not for me.
> I want for my part

Only the little white rose of Scotland
That smells sharp and sweet – and breaks the heart.[5]

Like Geddes, MacDiarmid was a maelstrom of ideas and his renaissance was to fire on all intellectual cylinders with some controversial sparks and bangs. Yet, though some of MacDiarmid's later poems seem overloaded by his omnivorous reading, it is as a poet that he provides a unique cutting edge to Scotland's modern literature. His early lyrics are simultaneously metaphysical and intimate, while his profound use of Scots evokes nature near and far, as in 'The Bonnie Broukit Bairn'.

Mars is braw in crammasy (crimson),
Venus in a green silk goun,
The auld mune shak's her gowden feathers,
Their starry talk's a wheen o' blethers,
Nane for thee a thochtie sparin'
Earth, thou bonnie broukit (neglected) bairn![6]

Voice and perspective are both original, and we see familiar things afresh, as in 'The Eemis Stane', which is a tomb stone eroded by time.

I' the how-dumb-deid o' the cauld hairst nicht
The warl' like an eemis stane
Wags i' the lift (sky);
An' my eerie memories fa'
Like a yowdendrift (whirling snow drift).[7]

But these resonant, crafted lyrics could not contain MacDiarmid's vision, and in 1926 he published *A Drunk Man Looks at the Thistle*, which is a modernist masterwork in a distinctively Scottish mode. On one level this long poem is about the narrator's struggle to get home from the pub, directly echoing Robert Burns' 'Tam o' Shanter', whose hero is also torn between imaginative vision and domestic reality. But around his narrator's ground-level encounter with the thistle, MacDiarmid weaves a dramatic flow of reflection and polemic, gathering like waves into lyric intensity. Everything is unified by one purpose embodied in the spiky plant.

> Whatever Scotland is to me,
> Be it aye pairt o aa men see
> O Earth and o Eternity[8]

Scotland can only be truly seen in 'true scale' to the infinite. This requires knowledge but also vision in the tradition of Thomas the Rhymer.

> Oor universe is like an ee
> Turned in man's benmaist hert to see
> And swamped in subjectivity.[9]

But that enquiry also leads to a turning outward, synthesising subjective and objective, until Scotland is brought into universal focus. 'The thistle yet'll unite / Man and the Infinite!'

A Drunk Man Looks at the Thistle can also be heard as a dramatic monologue, and was successfully performed by the actor Tom Fleming.

> Jean! Janet! Gin she's no here it's no oor bed,
> Or else I'm dreamin' deep and canna wauken,
> But it's a fell queer dream if this is no'
> A real hillside – and those things thistle and
> bracken![10]

The publication of the poem was in itself a dramatic event. Apart from those explicitly attacked – kirks without Christianity and Burns Clubs without Burns – MacDiarmid's voice aroused passionate support and disagreement from then onwards. If only he could have gone on producing perfect lyrics, some wondered wistfully, but that was not MacDiarmid as a personality or poet.

Controversy, however, can distract, and MacDiarmid's poetic achievement is substantial. He went on to produce a contemplative masterwork *On A Raised Beach* in experimental English. Despite his love of long poems, MacDiarmid also remained able to express himself with eloquence and concision, as in the later poem 'A Point in Time', written in response to William Johnstone's painting of that name.

> Now you understand how stars and hearts are one
>   with another [...]
> How the boundless dwells perfect and undivided in
>   the spirit,
> How each part can be infinitely great and infinitely
>   small[11]

The poet continues in what is at the deepest level a cosmic and religious vision.

> How the utmost extension is but a point, and how
> Light, harmony, movement, power
> All identical, all separate, and all united are life.[12]

In the end, MacDiarmid's self-assessment in his poem 'Scotland' rings true.

> So I have gathered unto myself
> all the loose ends of Scotland,
> and by naming them, and accepting them,
> loving them and identifying myself with them,
> attempt to express the whole.[13]

The Capital Scene

Hugh MacDiarmid was a Scottish Borderer from Langholm, and through his long creative life he moved away from cities. The Renaissance he inspired was shaped in Montrose, the Borders, Sutherland, Orkney and Shetland, as well as Glasgow and Edinburgh. Yet the capital city still played an important role. It was the stage set of Scotland's political and cultural history. Edwin Muir reflected bleakly on the gap between Edinburgh's 'legendary past and its tawdry present' in a visit in 1935, as part of his *Scottish Journey*. The land, he wrote in what became 'Scotland's Winter', was 'kingless' and 'songless'.

But even as Muir wrote these words, the city was stirring with new combinations of personality and talent. MacDiarmid came to Edinburgh to study at the Broughton High School Student Centre, where he was stimulated and encouraged by his teacher,

George Ogilvie. Sorley MacLean came from Raasay and Skye to study at Edinburgh University, where he met two profound young thinkers about Scotland – George Davie and James Caird. They encouraged him to write in his native Gaelic, and he met and assisted MacDiarmid with the Scots poet's new translations of important Gaelic poems. In the late '30s, MacLean returned to Edinburgh to become Head of English at Boroughmuir High School.

Sorley MacLean's poetry of this period matches MacDiarmid in its blend of national and international, its originality and its linguistic distinctiveness. But Maclean has his own way of combining the personal, political and metaphysical. This early poem from his defining sequence *Dàin do Eimhir* begins like a traditional Gaelic love poem – 'Girl of the yellow, heavy-yellow, gold-yellow hair' – but moves seamlessly into the contemporary.

> Would your song and splendid beauty take
> from me the dead loathsomeness of these ways,
> the brute and the brigand at the head of Europe
> and your mouth red and proud with the old song?
>
> An tugadh t' fhonn no t' àilleachd ghlòrmhor
> Bhumsa gràinealachd mharbh nan dòigh seo,
> A' bhrùid's am meàirleach air ceann na h-Eòrpa
> 's do bhial-sa uaill-dhearg san t-seann òran?[14]

The concentration and stark power of MacLean's poetry is evident as he brings together his emotions about the Spanish Civil War and two unhappy love affairs, in verse that stands on its own unique ground.

What would the kiss of your proud mouth be
compared with each drop of the precious blood
that fell on the cold frozen uplands
of Spanish mountains from a column of steel?

Dè bhiodh pòg do bheòil uaibhraich
Mar ris gach braon den fhuil luachmhoir
A thuit air raointean reòta fuara
Nam bean Spàinnteach bho fhòirne cruadhach?[15]

Dáin do Eimhir stands alongside *A Drunk Man Looks at the Thistle* as a defining work of the 20th century literary Renaissance, and MacLean acknowledges Edinburgh in an apt way within the sequence.

Often when I called Edinburgh
a grey town without darting sun,
it would light up your beauty,
a refulgent, white-starred town.
Tric 's mi gabhail air Dùn Èideann
baile glas gun ghathadh grèine,
's ann a lasadh e led bhòidhche,
baile lòghmhor geal-reultach.[16]

Alongside these profound achievements, there was also a performative staginess at work in the Renaissance, and Edinburgh was its theatre of choice. Writers rehearsed new identities and, to a degree, performed them. Hugh MacDiarmid was the penname of Christopher Murray Grieve, who also features as Hugh Skene in Eric Linklater's satiric novel *Magnus Merriman*, partly set in the city. The poets met in venues such as Milne's Bar, the Café Royal and the Abbotsford, which Alexander Moffat combines in his group portrait 'Poets' Pub'. There was a self-consciousness of the new that required an element of show. There was also a 'male club' element in the 20s and 30s, but fortunately women writers, including Helen Cruikshank, Willa Muir, Violet Jacob, Nan Shepherd and Naomi Mitchison, soon widened and deepened the movement.

The Edinburgh Stage

The Scottish cultural Renaissance arose in reaction to World War I. The appalling loss of life left Scotland in mourning with an inheritance of lives shattered by grief and disability. The British Empire came under question from both socialists and Scottish nationalists. Led by the Duke of Atholl, Scotland created its own National War Memorial in Edinburgh Castle which enabled an outpouring of sorrow, as well as some glimmers of comfort through its inclusiveness and dignified solidarity.

World War II was a different experience as people reluctantly took up arms against the menace of fascism. Through the war, Scotland's political and cultural identity strengthened towards post-war reconstruction. Amidst this came increased opportunities in the professional arts and a determination to widen the Renaissance. In this mood of recovery, the idea emerged of holding an international festival of the arts in Edinburgh. The city was relatively unscathed from the war and had a strong European identity. Where better to raise a cultural flag for peace and reconstruction?

This was essentially the idea of Henry Harvey Wood, the British Council representative in his hometown. But to make things happen, it also took the creative entrepreneurship of Rudolph Bing, who had escaped his native Vienna by the skin of his teeth after the Nazi takeover. Bing was looking for somewhere for the Glyndebourne Opera to perform while its own home base was closed. Finally it took a Tory Lord Provost, John Falconer, to see the practical benefits and to back the fledgling venture with essential cash.

The first Edinburgh International Festival of Music and Drama was staged in 1947. It presented top-class opera and music in the King's Theatre and Usher Hall, top-class ballet at the Playhouse Theatre, French drama at the Royal Lyceum Theatre, a series of films organised by the Edinburgh Film Guild, piping and dance on the Castle Esplanade and, by special relaxation of rationing, the illumination of the Castle for four nights.

A new work by Scottish playwright James Bridie had been planned, but did not come together in time. This omission became a slight when Bing turned down offers from emergent Scottish companies such as Glasgow Unity to perform at their own risk, on the grounds that they were not of sufficient quality. Maybe, riposted Unity, their accents did not fit with those of the Old Vic. Bridie took up the public cudgels saying Glasgow Unity were welcome to appear in Edinburgh, but should not try and compete at a level they did not understand! Next up Hugh MacDiarmid, always good for a stramash, pronounced that Scotland could not progress culturally 'by taking in our neighbours' washing'.

There was more heat than light, but the arguments did have a positive effect with the emergence of a high-quality Festival

Fringe. Glasgow Unity performed at the Little Theatre in The Pleasance, the Scottish Community Drama Association produced Bridie's *The Anatomist*, and the Carnegie Trust supported *Everyman* at Dunfermline Abbey. The recently opened Gateway Theatre in Leith Walk aligned with the official Festival, hosting TS Eliot's *Murder in the Cathedral* and *The Family Reunion*. The remarkable thing was that all these ventures, official and unofficial, were successful.

The hunt was then on for a 1948 Scottish drama in the official programme. The key movers were Bridie, Tyrone Guthrie of the Old Vic (who had worked with Bridie in the pre-war Scottish National Players), and the Gateway Theatre. The bold concept was to mount the first modern production of David Lindsay's *Ane Satire of the Thrie Estaitis* in a new adaptation by journalist and playwright Robert Kemp. But where? Guthrie wanted a non-conventional theatre space.

By some alchemy, the idea emerged of using the Church of Scotland General Assembly Hall. The Gateway was owned by the Church, and its redoubtable manager Sadie Aitken made the vital connections. Almost unnoticed, religious opposition to the arts had evaporated to be replaced by enlightened encouragement. The Assembly Hall was as near to an Elizabethan thrust stage, with timber galleries on four sides, as any modern building could offer. After a hesitant start the production became a runaway success, reviving Scotland's European connections and the vigorous talent base of its emergent professional theatre. Despite continuing disagreements about the official Festival's role, it was clear that the Festivals phenomenon was of huge benefit to Scottish arts and culture.

Of course this had not happened overnight. In her defining Edinburgh novel, *The Prime of Miss Jean Brodie*, Muriel Spark recalls concerts, theatre, ballet and literary readings in the 1930s. Spark resisted autobiographical connections in her fiction, but made an exception of Jean Brodie, who is based on her own Edinburgh teacher Christina Kay. Despite affairs and her admiration for Mussolini, Miss Brodie's prevailing passion is to bring on her young favourites through cultural experiences.

Published in 1961, the novel is entertaining and subtle, since Miss Brodie has a Calvinist-style conviction that God is on her side. Yet in reality Calvin is being upended in Morningside, the heart of Edinburgh's middle-class morals and churchgoing, by a very determined, self-justified sinner, ready even to cross boundaries between her lovers and her pupils. 'She was an Edinburgh Festival all on her own' recalls one of her fictional girls, pinpointing the role of the Festivals in this wider revolution. A major shift had occurred in the psychological and social mood, and they provided an arena for innovation.

In 1959, Jim Haynes, a young American who had come to Kirknewton Airfield, opened the Paperback Bookshop in Charles Street close to George Square. A rhinoceros head, which was Haynes' shop sign (strangely anticipating the surreal Ionesco play) still marks the spot on a modern University block, though without explanation. The bookshop, like the Laigh Coffee House in the New Town owned by actor Moultrie Kelsall, signalled the city's more confident mood.

The Paperback Bookshop hosted events and opened up a gallery space in the cellar where Richard Demarco organised his first exhibition. Among its early Fringe performances were readings of

David Hume's *Dialogues Concerning Natural Religion*, and *Ane Tryall of Hereticks* which was from a novel-in-progress by Fionn MacColla, author of *And the Cock Crew*, a powerful inditement of post-Reformation Scotland.

Among those organising author events was radical publisher John Calder, who proposed an International Writers Conference to the Edinburgh Festival. This was endorsed by its new Director, Lord Harewood, and the first event took place in 1962, with a heady mix of Scottish and international talent selling out the McEwan Hall. Loosely themed around 'The Novel', topics included censorship, homosexuality and what came to be known as the beat writers.

But the event became notorious due to an unseemly barney on the second day between a new generation gay talent Alexander Trocchi, author of *Cain's Book*, and Hugh MacDiarmid. In the heat of debate, and likely under the influence of drugs, Trocchi denounced the last decade of Scottish literature, apart from his own contribution, as stale, parochial porridge. MacDiarmid responded by denouncing homosexuality and lesbianism as beneath the attention of serious writers. Likely under the influence of alcohol, he reportedly described Trocchi offstage as 'metropolitan scum'. Other contributors, including Muriel Spark and Edwin Morgan, tried to defuse the atmosphere, but the spat seized press and public interest. The whole event ended with an all-night New Town party at which Norman Mailer assaulted the translator Max Hayward for being over-friendly with Sonia Orwell, who had helped Calder organise the conference.

Harewood was delighted and wanted more, so theatre was set as the 1963 theme, with Calder and drama critic Kenneth

Tynan as co-organisers. This proved an even larger gathering but surprisingly a much duller affair, until the last session. There was to be a pre-planned Happening, but both the planning and the Happening became chaotic, culminating in a topless model being wheeled across the platform in full view. The press went wild as did some Town Councillors who, in the absence of Presbyterian fervour, still harboured a form of civic prudery. Calder and the model were tried for indecency but acquitted. Harewood had to resign as Director due to an unrelated divorce. The 1964 conference on poetry was cancelled.

Meanwhile, in 1963, Jim Haynes and Richard Demarco became involved in opening the Traverse Theatre Club in James Court off the High Street. The premises were a former brothel nicknamed 'Hell's Kitchen'. The resultant studio theatre space was ideal for experimental work, and as a private club it was free from censorship by the Lord Chamberlain. The subsequent move to the Grassmarket kept The Traverse alive as a year-round crucible for new writing, and a prime Fringe venue for decades to come. Edinburgh was becoming more like its festivals.

Culture and Politics

Economic growth and the expansion of higher education in the '60s brought a new wave of opportunity in the arts, across the barriers of social class. At the same time, controversies about censorship, sexuality, drugs, socialism, feminism, nuclear weapons and the Vietnam War kept culture on the cutting edge of change. There was optimism and hope for humanity.

This mood quickly evaporated as the 1970s went into crisis mode. Energy shortages, strikes, inflation, conflict in Northern Ireland and disagreement about joining the European Economic Community created instability. Nationalism surged in Scotland, challenging the political *status quo*. In 1979 a Devolution Referendum took place, but the majority vote was disallowed because 60 per cent of the total electorate had not turned out to vote 'yes'. A few months later Margaret Thatcher was elected Prime minister of the UK, inaugurating 17 years of increasingly unpopular Conservative rule in Scotland.

In many ways the divisive '70s set the political dynamic for the next 50 years. The Tories were ousted in 1997 and a second Devolution Referendum was overwhelmingly carried, leading to a restored Scottish Parliament rather than the lesser Assembly proposed in 1979. But the rise of national feeling continued with the Scottish National Party unexpectedly forming a minority and then majority government. In 2014 David Cameron, the UK Prime Minister conceded an Independence Referendum which voted 55 per cent to 45 per cent to remain in the UK. Emboldened by this win, Cameron followed with a Referendum on EU membership which he lost in 2016, resulting in a calamitous hard Brexit, and huge disaffection in Scotland which had voted with a two thirds majority to stay in the European Union. Scotland's sense of itself as a small European nation, rather than the first fruits of the British Empire, was dealt a severe blow as Brexit Britain set about strengthening the UK nation state at the expense of devolution.

Yet through these twists and turns, still ongoing, the cultural Renaissance continued, exhibiting different overlapping features in different writers. The MacDiarmid project to see Scotland in-the-round internationally was a success, gradually overcoming the lack of education or media coverage as regards Scottish culture. Many Scots had possessed only a partial view of their own country, conditioned by class, locality or even religion.

There was also a resistance mode in Scottish writing, which kicked in from the democracy denial of 1979. This ranged from outright protest, as in the plays of John McGrath and 7:84 Scotland, to imaginings of different possible societies – all feeding off the idea that a nation is an imagined community. 'Work now as if you were in the early days of a better nation', coined novelist Alasdair Gray, adapting Geddes style from earlier writers. Playwrights such as Stewart Conn, Donald Campbell and Hector MacMillan turned to history as a source of reimagining.

What united these approaches was a new cultural confidence, long seeded by folksong collector and poet Hamish Henderson in his 'Freedom Come All Ye' anthem. Divided selves gave way to clear-eyed views of Scotland's problems – poverty, addiction, bigotry and fatalism – on the basis that change was possible and potentially in our own hands.

Another feature of this confidence was the sheer number of writers and artists working in Scotland, led now from the urban west. Authors as varied as Edwin Morgan, Robin Jenkins, Stewart Conn, Agnes Owens, James Kelman, Liz Lochhead, Tom Leonard, Janice Galloway, Alan Spence and Jackie Kay, to name a few, overlapped with and supported each other. Edinburgh followed on with genre breakthroughs by Ian Rankin and Alexander McCall Smith in detective fiction, JK Rowling in children's fantasy, James Robertson in historical fiction such as *Joseph Knight* and Irvine Welsh with *Trainspotting*, an urban novel for Edinburgh.

However, it is unfair on writers and readers to simply list names.

Literary histories by Robert Crawford and Alan Riach offer detailed surveys of this period. Instead, I want to return to the main character of this book, Edinburgh itself.

City of Literature

Edinburgh has worn different disguises: a mythic location, the stage set for history, a Puritan town, a divided city, a festive capital. Without entirely shedding any of these identities, late 20th and early 21st-century Edinburgh experienced its own flowering. The city is home to writers, illustrators, designers, publishers, translators, theatre makers, film producers, multimedia creators, broadcasters and researchers. A swathe of literary organisations run through the city from the National Library of Scotland to the Saltire Society, Scottish Book Trust, the Scottish Poetry Library, Edinburgh International Book Festival, Scottish Pen, the Scottish Storytelling Centre and the Scottish Publishers Association.

Many genres of writing in a diversity of languages flourish in the city, from children's literature to crime writing, historical fiction to life writing, science and environmental writing, comic novels and podcasts. In 2004, in recognition of all this Edinburgh was designated the first UNESCO City of Literature, generating a network that now covers 53 cities in nine continents. Where will all that go in face of economic and political challenges? As ever, Edinburgh awaits new directions, fresh energy.

For now we should enjoy the city's literary delights in virtual or real time. In Makars Court beside The Writers Museum, every paving stone gives voice to writers past and present. From there you can descend in full view of the astonishing Walter Scott

Monument and proceed by way of Allan Ramsay's statue to the Scottish National Portrait Gallery, and the Stevenson family home in Heriot Row. Alternatively, you can go out onto the High Street, past Robert Burns' first lodgings and cross to Geddes' Riddle's Court. Or going down the High Street you encounter Alexander Stoddart's statue of David Hume in a classical toga, and Adam Smith surrounded by symbols of industry.

Heading from the High Street into the Canongate, you can follow Robert Fergusson down to the Scottish Parliament, where a wall of poems and quotations rounds off the Royal Mile. 'If a man were permitted to make all the ballads of a nation,' intones the parliamentarian Fletcher of Saltoun, 'he need not care who makes the laws of a nation.' And luminous poet Norman MacCaig reaches from Edinburgh to Sutherland and back:

> Who possesses this landscape?
> The man who bought it or
> I who am possessed by it?[17]

That perception seems especially fitting for a Scottish Parliament building that looks to sea and land. The bold design by Catalan architect Enric Miralles runs out from Holyrood towards the Salisbury Crags and finally the sea. It has had as great an impact on Edinburgh's townscape as the restoration of the Parliament on Scotland's politics.

The cancelled Scottish Assembly of 1979 was to have met in the Old Royal High School on Calton Hill. This building was again considered in 1999, along with a number of other potential sites and outline designs. In the meantime, Parliament convened in the Kirk's General Assembly Hall, tuning in perhaps to David Lindsay's John Commonweal urging reform.

The key decision maker on the new building was Donald Dewar, the first First Minister of Scotland. A Glasgow lawyer and Labour devolutionist, Dewar was a serious politician who counted George Buchanan among his favourite authors. But Dewar harboured creative imagination, being from childhood a frequent Edinburgh Festivals attender. He recognised the dramatic boldness of Miralles' design for the Holyrood site, and cast caution to the winds, channelling national and international aspiration into a vivid form on a site associated with Scottish nationhood for 900 years. The project was to poise enormous challenges for the fledgling Parliament, including Miralles' and Dewar's tragic deaths, but the end result is a world-ranking masterpiece.

Why this matters is brilliantly expressed in 'Open the Doors!', Edwin Morgan's poem for the opening of the building in 2004. This was the same year in which he was appointed Scotland's first Makar or National Poet, and Edinburgh became the world's first City of Literature.

> Open the doors! Light of the day, shine in; light of
>   the mind, shine out!
> We have a building which is more than a building.
> There is a commerce between inner and outer,
> between brightness and shadow,
> between the world and those who think about the world.

It is an Enlightenment invocation, yet like Geddes Morgan acknowledges the mysteries of form and art.

> Is it not a mystery? The parts cohere, they come
>   together like petals of a flower,
> yet they also send their tongues outward to feel and
>   taste the teeming earth.

But the building makes it a people's house of surprises – 'imperial marble it is not!'

> Did you want classic columns and predictable
>   pediments? A growl of old Gothic
> grandeur? A blissfully boring box?
> Not here, no thanks! No icon, no IKEA, no iceberg,
>   but curves and caverns, nooks
> and niches, huddles and heavens, syncopations and
>   surprises. Leave
> symmetry to the cemetery.

And how do you get there? Down the Royal Mile past 'the closes and wynds of the noted ghosts of history', and before them 'the auld makars who tickled a Scottish king's ear with melody and ribaldry and frank advice'. And then this from a deeply Glaswegian poet:

> This is where you know your parliament should be
> And this is where it is, just here.[18]

In conclusion Morgan delivers some frank advice of his own. The politicians must match the building they have been given. What people do not want, and here John Commonweal speaks again, is 'a nest of fearties', 'a symposium of procrastinators', 'a phalanx of forelock-tuggers' and 'above all the droopy mantra of "it wizny me"'.

There is political realism in this address, as Morgan reminds the lawgivers that they are picking up an almost lost thread 'of pride and self-esteem' yet, 'with a sense of not wholly the power, not yet wholly the power'. But there is the future and everything to play for. 'So now begin. Open the doors and begin.'

As read on the day by Liz Lochhead, this exemplified poetry as public speech, just as Sheena Wellington's rendition of Robert Burns' 'A Man's a Man for A' That' delivered poetry as public song. Few parliaments in the world can have opened with such literary garlands, even if partly woven with thistles.

Another level had been raised on Edinburgh's storied town.

Conclusion

THE NEARER WE come to the present, the harder it is to see the wood for the trees. Future readers and writers will decide what is of enduring value. Some important figures in this book were not fully appreciated in their own lifetimes, while other writers – celebrities of their time – now barely rate a mention.

Literature is an act of lasting freedom which should not be constrained by critical orthodoxies, marketing brands or ideologies of race, religion, gender or class. Yet, equally, literature cannot be solely an individual affair. Language works through collective evolution and shared understandings. Literary voices are distinctive but collaborative with past, present and future writing. I have tried to trace some of those continuities along with the innovations.

However, I would go further. A city of literature needs friendship and mutual support. That has been my experience of working in Edinburgh for 50 years. That spirit recognises and nurtures talent, from creative early learning through to international awards. Only the citizens of Edinburgh can sustain such an ethos, so the future is in all our hands.

But the future looks difficult. Creative innovation and the solidarity of shared understandings are needed as never before. Literature has begun to seed a future in which human life can be reintegrated with the natural life of planet earth, our common home. The shift of consciousness, anticipated by Patrick Geddes, has become vital. A city by the sea, a city of ideas – our writers are midwives of human ecology.

When he came to the end of his monumental *Scotichronicon*

on Inchcolm, Walter Bower was profoundly relieved that his ship had safely reached harbour. Our future voyage has only just begun. Blessed be the ship and all who sail in her.

Timeline

THIS SUMMARY TIMELINE interleaves historical events with important literary milestones. It is a convenient guide to where authors sit chronologically, and shows interesting connections between books and events.

597	Death of Columba on Iona *The Gododdin* of Aneirin
638	Anglo-Saxons capture Edinburgh
700	Adomnan's *Life of Columba*
798	Norse raids on Scotland begin
1057	Death of King Macbeth
1097	Death of Queen Margaret Turgot's *Life of Saint Margaret*
1124	David I becomes King Edinburgh confirmed as royal burgh
1130	*Orkneyinga Saga*
1263	Battle of Largs *Heimskringla* of Snorri Sturluson
1286	Death of Alexander III Prophecies of Thomas the Rhymer
1297	Edward I annexes Scotland
1305	Execution of William Wallace
1314	Battle of Bannockburn

1320	Declaration of Arbroath
1360	Fordun's Chronicle
1412	University of St Andrews founded
1424	James I freed from England *The Kingis Quair*/Wyntoun's Chronicle
1440–7	Bower's *Scotichronicon*
1460–1500	Poems of Robert Henryson
1477	Blind Harry's *The Wallace*
1503	James IV marries Margaret Tudor
1507	First printing press in Edinburgh
1513	Battle of Flodden
1527	Boece's History of the Scots
1532	Court of Session founded
1542	Death of James V George Buchanan emerges as poet
1546	George Wishart executed
1546	Cardinal Beaton assassinated
1552	*Satire of the Thrie Estaitis* performed
1560	Scottish Reformation Begins Geneva Bible completed
1561	Queen Mary returns to Scotland
1563	John Knox resumes his *History*

1567	Assassination of Darnley
1571	Buchanan's *Detection of Mary*
1572	Death of John Knox
1579	Buchanan's *De Jure Regni*
1582	Buchanan's *History* printed and burned
1587	Execution of Mary in England
1603	Union of the Crowns
1603–49	Poems of William Drummond
1611	King James Bible completed
1638	The National Covenant
1638–50	Poems of Montrose
1650	Execution of Charles I and Execution of Montrose
1650–61	Works of Thomas Urquhart
1651	Oliver Cromwell annexes Scotland
1661	Restoration of Charles II
1661–90	Covenanter resistance
1683	James Sutherland's *Hortus Medicus*
1688–9	'Glorious' Revolution
1689	Battle of Killiecrankie
1690	Robert Kirk's Gaelic Bible and *The Secret Commonwealth*
1698–9	Darien Expeditions

1707	Union of the Parliaments
1715	Jacobite Rising
1715–35	Poems of Allan Ramsay
1736–7	Theatre in Carrubbers Close
1736	The Porteous Riots
1740	David Hume's *Treatise of Human Nature*
1745–6	Jacobite Rising
1756	John Home's *Douglas*
1759	Adam Smith's *Theory of Moral Sentiments*
1760–5	Macpherson's *Poems of Ossian*
1767	Edinburgh's New Town begins
1770–4	Poems of Robert Fergusson
1771	*Encylopaedia Britannica* printed
1773	Boswell and Johnson's tour
1776	Adam Smith's *Wealth of Nations*
1785	James Hutton's *Theory of the Earth*
1786	Robert Burns' Kilmarnock Edition
1786–8	Burns based in Edinburgh
1787	The Scots Musical Museum begins
1789	The French Revolution
1791	First Statistical Account of Scotland

1802	*Edinburgh Review* launched
1805–17	Poems of Sir Walter Scott
1814	Battle of Waterloo Scott's *Waverley* published
1817	*Blackwood's Magazine* launched
1822	George IV visits Scotland
1827–75	Works of Thomas Carlyle
1832	First Franchise Reform Act Death of Sir Walter Scott
1843	Disruption of Church of Scotland
1848	European Revolutions
1849–97	Works of Margaret Oliphant
1879–94	Works of Robert Louis Stevenson
1887	Conan Doyle's A Study in Scarlet
1890	Forth Railway Bridge completed
1901	Death of Queen Victoria
1904	JM Barrie's *Peter Pan* produced
1914–8	World War I
1926	*A Drunk Man Looks at the Thistle*
1932	Death of Patrick Geddes
1939–45	World War II

1947	First Edinburgh International Festival and Festival Fringe
1948	*Ane Satyre of the Thrie Estaitis* produced
1952–2010	Poems of Edwin Morgan
1960	Hamish Henderson's 'Freedom Come All Ye'
1961	Muriel Spark's *Prime of Miss Jean Brodie* George Davie's *The Democratic Intellect*
1962–3	International Writers Conferences
1963	Traverse Theatre Club opens
1964	Forth Road Bridge completed
1973	*Cheviot, the Stag and the Black, Black Oil*
1979	First Devolution Referendum
1979	Margaret Thatcher becomes PM
1981	Alasdair Gray's *Lanark*
1983	First Edinburgh International Book Festival
1984	Scottish Poetry Library opens
1993	Irvine Welsh's *Trainspotting*
1997	Second Devolution Referendum
1999	Scottish Parliament Reconvenes
2001	Scottish Storytelling Centre established
2002	Stewart Conn first Edinburgh Makar

2004	Scottish Parliament building opens Wall of Poems at Parliament Edwin Morgan first national Makar Edinburgh first World City of Literature
2005	Valerie Gillies Edinburgh Makar
2008, 2011	Ron Butlin Edinburgh Makar
2011	Liz Lochhead national Makar
2014	Scottish Independence Referendum Christine De Luca Edinburgh Makar
2016	Brexit Referendum Jackie Kay national Makar
2017	Queensferry Crossing completed Alan Spence Edinburgh Makar
2020–2	Covid Pandemic
2021	Kathleen Jamie national Makar Hannah Lavery Edinburgh Makar
2022	Queen Elizabeth dies Scotland's Year of Stories

Further Reading

HERE ARE SOME suggestions and sources for further exploration.

Follow up your own interests in specific writers to find fresh perspectives. Explore the Highlands through the novels of Neil M Gunn, or contemporary Scotland through women writers, from novelist, short story writer and stand-up comedian AL Kennedy to poet, environmental essayist and national Makar Kathleen Jamie. A wide range of individual Scottish writers are in print and/or available second-hand or on the web.

Look at www.booksfromscotland.com which has a wide selection of books produced by Scottish publishers. There are some excellent anthologies, such as Roderick Watson's *The Poetry of Scotland: Gaelic, Scots and English* (Edinburgh University Press, 1995) or Catherine Kerrigan's *An Anthology of Scottish Women Poets* (Edinburgh University Press, 1991). The Association for Scottish Literature (www.asl.org.uk) produces new editions of interesting works and anthologies. William Hamilton's translation of Blind Harry's *The Wallace* has been published by Luath Press with a comprehensive introduction by Elspeth King.

For literary histories and surveys, there is a four-volume *History of Scottish Literature* edited by Cairns Craig for Aberdeen University Press, *The Edinburgh Companions to Scottish Literature* produced by Edinburgh University Press and ASL's *International Companions to Scottish Literature*. There are also two recent one-volume surveys: Robert Crawford's *Scotland's Books* (Penguin Books, 2007) and Alan Riach's *Scottish Literature: An Introduction* (Luath Press, 2022). An *Oxford Companion to Scottish Theatre* is due for publication in 2025.

Endnotes

1   The closing poem from Walter Bower's *Scotichronicon* is quoted in English translation courtesy of the University of St Andrews Libraries and Museums. It can be accessed in *A History Book for Scots* (Birlinn, 2019).

2   *Apollos of the North* (ed) Robert Crawford (Polygon, 2006) p87

3   James Boswell's Journals – Thursday 20 January 1763 (Yale University Copyright)

4   JM Barrie *Peter Pan and Other Plays* (Oxford University Press, (1995) pp 136-7

5   Hugh MacDiarmid *Complete Poems 1920–1976* (Martin Brian and O'Keeffe, 1978) p17

6   Ibid p27

7   Ibid p86

8   Ibid p162

9   Ibid p163

10 Ibid p461

11 Ibid p652

12 Ibid p1069

13 Ibid p1069

14 Sorley MacLean's *From Wood to Ridge* (Carcanet/Birlinn, 1999) p9

15 Ibid p9

16 Ibid p11

17 Norman MacCaig *Collected Poems* (Chatto and Windus / The Hogarth Press, 1985) p214

18 Edwin Morgan's 'Open the Door!'(© Scottish Parliament), accessible on www.scottishpoetrylibrary.org.uk

Luath Press Limited

committed to publishing well written books worth reading

LUATH PRESS takes its name from Robert Burns, whose little collie Luath (*Gael.*, swift or nimble) tripped up Jean Armour at a wedding and gave him the chance to speak to the woman who was to be his wife and the abiding love of his life. Burns called one of the 'Twa Dogs' Luath after Cuchullin's hunting dog in Ossian's *Fingal*. Luath Press was established in 1981 in the heart of Burns country, and is now based a few steps up the road from Burns' first lodgings on Edinburgh's Royal Mile. Luath offers you distinctive writing with a hint of unexpected pleasures.

Most bookshops in the UK, the US, Canada, Australia, New Zealand and parts of Europe, either carry our books in stock or can order them for you. To order direct from us, please send a £sterling cheque, postal order, international money order or your credit card details (number, address of cardholder and expiry date) to us at the address below. Please add post and packing as follows: UK – £1.00 per delivery address; overseas surface mail – £2.50 per delivery address; overseas airmail – £3.50 for the first book to each delivery address, plus £1.00 for each additional book by airmail to the same address. If your order is a gift, we will happily enclose your card or message at no extra charge.

Luath Press Limited

543/2 Castlehill
The Royal Mile
Edinburgh EH1 2ND
Scotland
Telephone: 0131 225 4326 (24 hours)
Email: sales@luath.co.uk
Website: www.luath.co.uk